THE
OUTRUN

THE
OUTRUN

AMY LIPTROT

CANONGATE
Edinburgh · London

Published in Great Britain in 2016 by Canongate Books Ltd,
14 High Street, Edinburgh EH1 1TE

www.canongate.tv

3

British Library Cataloguing-in-Publication Data
A catalogue record for this book is available on
request from the British Library

ISBN 978 1 78211 547 2

Typeset in Bembo Std by Palimpsest Book Production Ltd,
Falkirk, Stirlingshire

Printed and bound in Great Britain by Clays Ltd, St Ives plc

MIX
Paper from
responsible sources
FSC   FSC® C018072
www.fsc.org

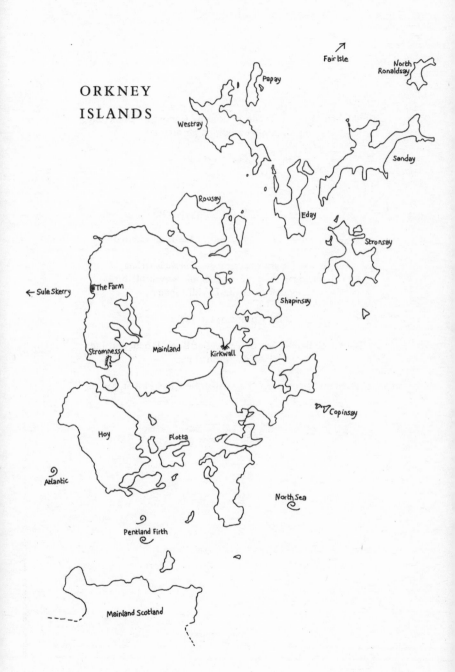

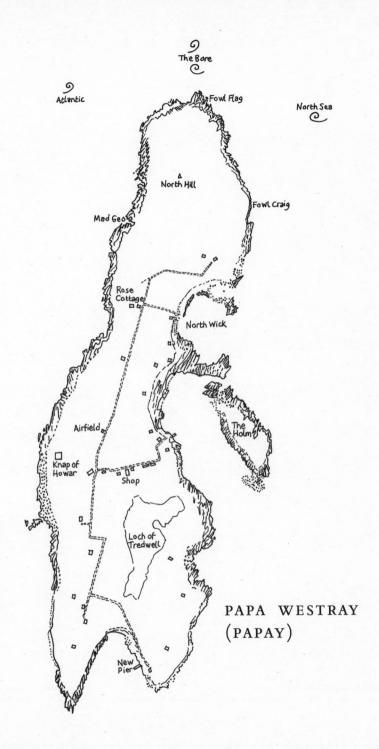

The Bore

Atlantic

Fowl Flag

North Sea

North Hill

Fowl Craig

Mad Geo

Rose Cottage

North Wick

Airfield

The Holm

Knap of Howar

Shop

Loch of Tredwell

PAPA WESTRAY (PAPAY)

New Pier

CONTENTS

GLOSSARY

bonxie: great skua

burn: stream

byre: barn

caddie lamb: orphan lamb, reared by bottle

clapshot: mashed mixed neeps and tatties

dyke: drystone wall

geo: narrow inlet of sea in cliffs

grimlins: midsummer night sky

haar: sea fog

hillyans: mythical hill folk

holm (pr. 'home'): offshore islet

kirk: church

kye: cattle

lum: chimney

lum reekin: chimney smoke

Merry Dancers: Northern Lights

midden: muck heap

muckle: big

neep: turnip

noust: hollow for storing small boats

peedie: small

selkie: seal

spoot: razor clam

steamer: ferry boat

steamin'/blazin'/guttered: drunk

steeves: stone structures for building stooks

stooks: stacks of grain

swappin' for auks: hunting seabirds

tangles: seaweed

tattie: potato

trows/trowies: trolls

teeicks: lapwings

tystie: black guillemot

whaups: curlews

yole: simple boat

UNDER WHIRRING HELICOPTER BLADES, A young woman holds her newborn baby as she is pushed in a wheelchair along the runway of the island airport to meet a man in a strait-jacket being pushed in a wheelchair from the other direction.

That day, the two twenty-eight-year-olds had been treated at the small hospital nearby. The woman was helped to deliver her first child. The man, shouting and out of control, was restrained and sedated.

Orkney – a group of islands at the north of Scotland, sea-scoured and wind-battered, between the North Sea and the Atlantic – has a good provision of services: hospital, airport, cinema, two secondary schools, a supermarket. One thing it does not have, however, is a secure unit for people certified mentally ill and a danger to themselves and others. If someone is sectioned under the Mental Health Act, they have to be taken south to Aberdeen.

Seen from above, from an aircraft carrying oil workers out to a rig or mail bags from mainland Scotland, the airport runway is a jolt on the open, treeless landscape. Regularly closing for days during high winds or sea fogs, it's where the daily drama of leaving and return is played out under air-traffic control, among the low-lying isles and far-reaching skies.

This May evening, as daisies shut their petals for the night, guillemots and kittiwakes return to the cliffs with sand eels for their chicks, and sheep shelter beside drystone dykes – it is my story's turn to unfold. As I arrive into this island world, my father is taken out of it. My birth, three weeks early, has brought on a manic episode.

My mum introduces the man – my dad – to his tiny daughter and briefly places me in his lap before he is taken into the aircraft and flown away. What she says to him is covered by the sound of the engine or carried off by the wind.

I

THE OUTRUN

O N MY FIRST DAY BACK I shelter beside an old freezer, down by some stinging nettles, and watch the weather approach over the sea. The waves crashing do not sound very different from the traffic in London.

The farm is on the west edge of the main and largest island in Orkney, on the same latitude as Oslo and St Petersburg, with nothing but cliffs and ocean between it and Canada. As agricultural practices changed, new buildings and machinery were added to the farm but the old sheds and tools remain, corroding in the salty air. A broken tractor shovel acts as a sheep trough. Stalls where cattle were once tied are now filled with defunct machinery and furniture that used to be in our house. In that byre I strung a rope swing from the rafters, and hung backwards by my knees over a gate that's now rusting into the ground.

To the south, the farm stretches along the shore to sandier land, which becomes the Bay of Skaill, a mile-long beach where the Stone Age village, Skara Brae, sits. To the north, the farm follows cliffs up to higher ground where heather grows. Each field has a prosaic name: 'front field', as you come up the track to the house; or 'lambing field', sheltered on all sides by drystone dykes. The largest of the fields, the 'Outrun', is a stretch of coastland at the top of the farm where the grass is always short, pummelled by wind and sea spray year-round. The Outrun is where the ewes and their lambs graze in summer after they are taken up from the nursery fields. It's where the Highland cattle overwinter, red and horned, running out under the huge sky.

Some historical agricultural records list farmland in two parts: the 'in-bye' arable land, close to the farm steading; and the 'out-bye' or 'outrun', uncultivated rough grazing further away, often on hillsides. In the past, outrun was sometimes used as communal grazing for a number of farms. This land is the furthest reaches of a farm, only semi-tamed, where domestic and wild animals co-exist and humans don't often visit so spirit people are free to roam. In Orcadian folklore, trowies are told to live in communities in mounds and hollows of the hills and there are tales of hillyans, little folk who emerge from the rough land to make mischief in the summer.

In a photo of the Outrun from the early eighties, I ride on Dad's shoulders as he and Mum show visiting English friends the desolate-seeming land they have bought. My parents wanted to buy a farm and kept travelling further north until they found one they could afford. Family and friends were surprised, and unsure if they could make it work, as were the locals. Orcadians had watched many idealistic southerners move to the islands only to leave after a couple of winters.

I grew up here next to these cliffs. I have never been afraid of heights. Dad would take us clifftop-walking as children. I'd shake free of Mum's hand and look over the edge at the churning water below. Grey flagstone – sheer drops and massive slabs – fringes the farm, and this monumental material and unforgiving forces formed the limits of the island and my world.

We had a dog once that went over. The collie pup set off chasing rabbits in a gale, did not notice the drop and was never seen again.

It's a windy day. I leave the shelter of the freezer and walk up to the Outrun for the first time in years, breathing deeply. There are no trees on the farm and in this open landscape there is an abundance of space.

All the rocks slope towards the sea. In my wellies, I walk along the cracks in the flagstones so I don't slip. Wisps of hair have blown free of my ponytail and are getting into my eyes and mouth, sticking to my face with sea spray, like when I was a kid and followed the sheepdogs, under gates and over dykes.

I find my favourite place: a slab of rock balanced at a precarious angle at the top of a cliff. I'd come here as a teenager, headphones on, dressed up and frustrated, looking out to the horizon, wanting to escape. From my spot on the stone I would watch the breakers crash, the gulls and fighter jets flying out over the sea.

On a clear day, south across the Pentland Firth, I can see the tips of the mountains of mainland Scotland from here: Ben Hope,

Ben Loyal, Cape Wrath. About the horizon's distance due west of the Outrun lies Sule Skerry, once home to Britain's most remote manned lighthouse. Out at sea, bobbing on the surface, I can make out wave-energy devices being tested by engineers. It's low tide and below me, at the base of the cliff, the rocks are exposed where a fishing boat came aground when I was eleven.

From my seat on the slab, I look north to the headland at Marwick, with its tower built in memorial to Lord Kitchener. In 1916, Kitchener died with 643 of his crew of 655 when HMS *Hampshire* went down two miles north-west of here, sunk by a mine from a German U-boat. Some of the twelve survivors were given shelter in the farmhouse that later would be ours.

In his account of the loss of the *Hampshire*, one survivor, W. M. Phillips, a sailor, vividly describes the night of the tragedy: 'I with my boots off, but otherwise fully clad, jumped, and with a last goodbye plunged into seething waters.' He was able to climb onto a large float and gives an account of how, since it was overloaded, those wearing lifebelts were 'asked to leave': 'With a few smiling remarks such as "We shall be there first", some 18 answered the call and plunged into the billows, thus sacrificing themselves to give their fellow shipmates their only possible chance of survival.'

After many hours when the sailors feared being dashed to their deaths on the rocks, the float came ashore in one of the geos – Nebbi Geo – on the Outrun. Walking this stretch of coast, I imagine the raft, as Phillips described, 'wedged in between the cliffs as if human hands had placed it there'. I picture farmers of the time searching the coastline in the dark for survivors, and the bodies of sailors strewn on the rocks.

The wind in Orkney is almost constant. At the farm, the westerly gales are the worst, bringing the sea with them, and tonnes of rock can be moved overnight, the map altered in the morning. Easterlies can be the most beautiful – when the wind blows towards the tide and skims a glittering canopy of spray from the top of the waves, catching the sun. The old croft houses are squat and firm, like many Orcadian people, built to survive the strongest gales. That sturdy balance has not been bred into me: I am tall and gangly.

Following the familiar coast, I'm trying not to feel unstable. It's been more than a decade since I lived here and memories from my childhood are merging with more recent events: the things that brought me back to Orkney. As I struggle to open a wire gate, I remember what I repeated to my attacker: 'I am stronger than you.'

At the end of a winter the land is brown and washed-out and the Outrun seems barren, but I know its secrets. A broken-down and overgrown boundary dyke was found to date back to the Neolithic Age and some of the stones that make up the Ring of Brodgar six miles away were from a quarry just north of here. One similar stone lies broken on the hillside – perhaps dropped on the way to the circle four thousand years ago. I remember the colony of Arctic terns that nested here, dive-bombing our heads during the breeding season, swooping close enough for us to feel their wings. The endangered great yellow bumblebee is found here in the summer, pollinating the red clover; magic mushrooms grow in the autumn; and a rare type of seaweed, *Fucus distichus*, unique to wave-battered rocky northern shores, grows on the rocks all year round.

At the top of the Outrun there is a sea stack known as 'the Spord' or 'the Stack o' Roo', a tower-block-sized rock that was once part of the cliff but now stands alone. In the summer, puffins nest on the stack, along with fulmars, shags, black-backed gulls and ravens. Carefully avoiding rabbit holes, I used to clamber down a grass slope to a ledge, the best place to tuck myself in, look across to the stack and watch the bustling seabird society – fulmars noisily defending their nests and puffins returning from far out at sea.

There are no fences on the Outrun to keep the sheep off the rocks and cliffs. In the early years of the farm, Dad climbed down and rescued ewes that got stuck on ledges, but as the flock matured, geographical knowledge and foot-sureness was bred into the bloodline.

After recent rain, the burn that runs down to the sea is flowing, where my brother Tom and I played, pushing ourselves and the dogs under a small stone bridge. Oystercatchers and curlews made nests in the tracks left by the tractor and we'd chase and catch the chicks, feeling their soft, hotly beating bodies in our hands before letting them go.

I stop at the place where, when I was a kid, a neighbour left his new tractor running while he jumped out to open a gate and neglected to pull on the handbrake. He was turned the other way as the tractor began to roll, driverless, down the sloping field. He could not run fast enough to catch it as it accelerated and, with unstoppable force, the expensive machine plunged over the edge of the cliff and smashed into the Atlantic.

Later in the afternoon, I come back up to the Outrun to feed the Highland cattle, squeezing in next to Dad in the cab of his tractor, the way I used to when I was small. I still know where the bumps and dips in the land are so I can hold on tightly when necessary. Dad lowers the loader holding the silage bale into the ring-feeder and the kye gather around. It's already dark and I stay in the cab and watch him, lit by the tractor headlights, cutting the thin black plastic off the bale and pulling it away so they can eat. His hair is mainly white now, and although he wears a padded boiler suit almost year round, he no longer needs gloves.

The Outrun is tucked away behind a low hill and beside the coast, and in the right spot you can't see any houses or be seen from the road. Dad told me that when he was high, in a manic phase, he had slept out here. At the end of the day, crouched away from the wind beside the freezer again, rolling a cigarette and eyeing the livestock, I have become my father.

2

TREMORS

W HEN I GET BACK FROM my walk on the Outrun, instead of entering the farmhouse I go to the machinery paddock and open the door to the caravan where Dad now lives. The sheepdog waits outside for him and the horses have their heads over the gate, looking for hay. The old caravan is weighted down with concrete blocks against the wind. One of the windows was blown out in a gale last winter and has been patched up with a wooden sheet.

Inside, Dad is wearing his outdoor boiler suit, with baler twine and a penknife always in the pockets, over a jumper that Mum knitted, which he still wears, now patched at the elbows. He's sitting in the upholstered corner seat with the best view out through the large Perspex window, across the farmyard and fields, over the bay to a headland. The colours of the sky and the light on the sea change all day as rapid Atlantic weather systems pass over. When the clouds break, sunlight dazzles on the water. An outcrop of rock is exposed at low tides. Sometimes the light picks out in fine detail the hills of Hoy, another island to the south beyond the headland, and on other days they disappear completely in the haar.

In a shaft of winter sun, the air is dusty with muck from outside and smoke from the roll-ups Dad smokes. There are outdoor clothes and wellies by the door, farm paperwork spread over the low table, and the glow of a gas fire. At the other end of the caravan is a bedroom and the dog sleeps directly below Dad, under the caravan, like a wolf in its cave.

'Did you feel anything up there?' Dad asks, before beginning to tell me, although I've heard it before, about the tremors. This stretch of cliffs and beaches, where the mythical Mester Muckle Stoorworm is first said to have made himself known, where the people of Skara Brae eked out their lives and where HMS *Hampshire* was sunk, has mysteries.

Some people on the west coast of Orkney, including Dad, say they experience tremors or booms sometimes, low echoes that seem strong enough to vibrate the whole island while at the same time being quiet enough to make them wonder if they imagined it. 'You hardly hear it, but feel it more,' says Dad. 'It's a low-grade boom, like thunder at a distance. There are vibrations of the ground enough to shake windows and shelves. It lasts for one pulse and is often repeated a few times in a couple of hours.' Locals say they have felt the booms over many years but are unable to identify a pattern to their occurrence. They wonder if it is geographical, man-made, even supernatural – or if it happens at all.

To understand the tremors I have to look deep within Orkney's topography. The geology of the West Mainland coast, with high cliffs at Marwick, Yesnaby and Hoy, strewn with the sea stacks, sloping rocks and treacherous currents responsible for many shipwrecks, is the first place to look. It is possible that the booms and tremors are caused by wave action within caves deep below the fields. As a large wave travels into a dead-end cave, it traps and compresses air at high pressure. When the wave retreats, the air bubble explodes, causing a boom.

Others blame the tremors on the military, and sonic booms produced by jet aircraft. Around sixty miles from Orkney, on mainland Scotland, the Cape Wrath Ministry of Defence range is where the military train on and offshore. This sparsely populated area is one of the few places in the UK where the 'big stuff' can be detonated. Heavy air weapons would be the only thing that could send a sonic wave as far as Orkney but wind conditions would have to be perfect. High-speed aircraft can also cause sonic booms as, on dive-bombing runs, they descend into denser air, but although Dad sometimes sees and hears the planes, he says the tremors do not come at the same time. I wonder if other, harder to grasp, even ghostly, island forces could be at play. The legend of Assipattle and the Mester Muckle Stoorworm tells of a huge sea monster, so large it could wrap its body around the world and destroy cities with a flick of its tongue. A layabout called Assipattle dreamed of saving the world and got his chance when he killed the Stoorworm by stuffing a burning peat into its liver, cooking it slowly from the inside. Writhing in agony, the Stoorworm thrashed its head, knocking out hundreds of its teeth, which formed the islands of Orkney, Shetland and the Faroes. Dragging itself to the edge of the earth, it curled up and died, its smouldering body becoming Iceland – a country full of hot springs, geysers and volcanoes. That liver is still burning so maybe the Stoorworm isn't dead at all. A tentacle may still be twitching around these shores and the tremors may be the aftershocks of the monster's death-throes.

Talking to Dad about the tremors, I feel slightly nervous. Our conversations are normally limited to the farm – what jobs need to be done or the condition of the sheep and the land – so hearing him speak about uncanny sensations and strange geology makes me concerned that he might be getting high. Mum taught me to look for the signs. At first it could be exciting, with Dad talking a lot, full of optimism and energy, but this would bubble over into his making impulsive purchases, such as expensive rams or farm equipment, staying up all night and moving animals at four in the morning, then grandiose thoughts, with him feeling he could change time and control the weather.

On the floor of the caravan there's a stool I remember from the farmhouse that Dad made in the hospital when he was a teenager. He was fifteen when he was first diagnosed with manic depression, now known as bipolar disorder, and schizophrenic tendencies. Since then, periodically, he has ups and downs of varying amplitude. Our family life was rocked by the waves of life at its extremes, by the cycles of manic depression. As well as the incidents with sectioning and straitjackets, followed by time away in a psychiatric hospital, there were months when he stayed in bed without saying a word. Today Dad is buoyant but, on other occasions, if he's subdued, I worry it may signal the beginning of a period of depression and one of his long winters of inactivity.

Once, when I was about eleven, Dad was so ill that he went round the farmhouse smashing all the windows one by one. The wind flew through the rooms, whisking my schoolwork from my desk. When the doctor arrived with tranquillisers, followed by the police and an ambulance, I yelled at them to go away. He'd been taken by something beyond his control. As the sedatives kicked in, I crouched with my father in a corner of my bedroom, sharing a banana. 'You are my girl,' he said.

The rumblings of mental illness under my life were amplified by the presence of my mother's extreme religion and by the landscape I was born into, the continual, perceptible crashing of the sea at the edges. I read about the 'shoaling process' – how waves increase in height, then break as they reach shallower water near the shore. Energy never expires. The energy of waves, carried across the ocean, changes into noise and heat and vibrations that are absorbed into the land and passed through the generations.

Since his teens, Dad has been treated on fifty-six occasions with electroconvulsive therapy. Used in the most severe cases of mental illness, an electric shock is passed into the brain to induce a seizure. No one quite knows how or why it works but patients often report feeling better afterwards, at least temporarily.

Ripples were set off the day I was born, and although I moved far away, the seizures I began to experience as my drinking escalated felt as if the tremors had caught up with me too. In lonely London bedrooms or in toilets at nightclubs, my wrists and jaw would freeze and my limbs wouldn't respond as usual. The alcohol I'd been pouring into myself for years was like the repeated action of the waves on the cliffs and it was beginning to cause physical damage. Something was crumbling deep within my nervous system and shook my body in powerful pulses to the extent that I was frozen and drooling, until they eased off enough for me to pour another drink or rejoin the party.

3

FLOTTA

E VEN ON THE BRIGHTEST DAY in Orkney there is a cool breeze that comes in from the sea. It reminds us that we are on an island, although we call the biggest island in the archipelago the 'Mainland' while everything else is just 'south'. As soon as the agricultural shows are over at the beginning of August, so is summer, and there are regular gales for the rest of the year. Autumn is brief, there are few trees, and winter blows in quickly.

A decade ago, in a September equinox wind, I came home for a few months – a graduate unable to find a job in the city. It was the year my parents split up, like many people's do, and, like most, I didn't think it would happen to mine, although perhaps it's surprising that a manic depressive and a born-again Christian stayed together so long.

I was working as a cleaner at the oil terminal on the island of Flotta and took the workers' ferry across from the pier at

Houton every day at dawn. Since the early seventies, pipelines and tankers have brought crude oil to the terminal from North Sea oil fields, dark energy from below the seabed. The oil industry was a boost for Orkney and provides some of its best-paid jobs but the cleaners were at the bottom of the pile.

The commute was the best thing about the job. Each day I drove across the island at sunrise and returned at sunset. Misty pastels appeared as I accelerated over the horizon listening to Radio Orkney or drum-and-bass, framing the islands and reflecting in the water of Scapa Flow. There were electric reds and oranges in the evening, the same colour as the flare that burns off excess gas at the terminal and the lights on the oil tankers out at sea.

After work, when I took off my tabard but never quite got rid of the smell of bleach, I spent nights on my own – Mum had recently moved out and Dad was elsewhere – in the farmhouse where I grew up. I was alone in a house on the edge of a cliff, drinking and smoking at the kitchen table where we used to have family meals, doing a job I didn't want, phoning my far-away friends at midnight while drinking Dad's homebrew, as my family came apart around me. Sometimes I would finish one bottle of wine, then drive five miles to the nearest open shop to get another. The next day I'd get on the ferry, headphones on, hung-over, furious and hurting.

At the oil terminal, I had to clean workers' bedrooms, mop bathrooms, sweep corridors and make beds. I became familiar with different types of dirt: from sweat on sheets, unseen but smelt, to dry footprint mud, satisfyingly hooverable. Toothpaste flecks on mirrors revealed the enthusiastic brusher, and ash showed who had been smoking out of the window in a non-smoking area. Dry and wet poo, ably distinguished by my supervisor, required different cleaning methods, and pubic hairs were left coiled on toilet seats. Most of the rooms I cleaned contained partially drunk bottles of Irn-Bru and some had finger- and toenail clippings buried in the carpet.

I felt as if I had become a ghost, walking nameless corridors under buzzing lights carrying a mop. The world out there, down south, had forgotten about me, stuck on the island with the bin bags, struggling to get a laundry cart through swing doors on my own. I was the wall that had eyes, knowing if workers had slept in their beds last night. I was the shadowy figure, scuttling away when I heard footsteps. Being back in Orkney was a failure and I saw the cleaning job as simply a way to make money to leave again.

At eighteen, I couldn't wait to leave. I saw life on the farm as dirty, hard and badly paid. I wanted comfort, glamour and to be at the centre of things. I didn't understand people who said that they wanted to live in the country where they could see wildlife. People were more interesting than animals. In the winter, forced into ugly outdoor clothes to help muck out the livestock, I dreamed of the hot pulse of the city.

But in my student flat, I would mentally map the 150 acres of the farm onto the inner city, thousands of people in the space that contained just our family and animals. It drove me crazy that, in a block of flats, I was existing just metres from someone yet didn't know who they were. Other people were sleeping through thin walls to the left and right of me, above and below. I didn't talk much about Orkney to my new friends, but lying in bed on windy nights, the noise made me feel as if I was back in the stone farmhouse and I thought of the animals outside in the cold.

When I was in the south it was easiest for me to say that I was 'Scottish' or 'come from Orkney' but that was not what I would say to a real Orcadian. Although I was born in Orkney and lived there until I was eighteen, I don't have an Orcadian accent and my family is from England. My parents met when they were eighteen, at college in Manchester, where Dad was retaking the A levels he'd missed due to his first bouts of illness and Mum was studying business. Mum grew up on a farm in Somerset, Dad is the son of teachers from Lancashire and was brought up in a Mancunian suburb. It was visits to Mum's farm that made him decide to go to agricultural college. My parents have lived on the islands for more than thirty years, over half their lives, yet are still viewed as English, from 'south'.

Usually, English people think that my accent is Scottish and Scottish people think I am English. The old Orcadian way to ask someone where they come from: 'Where do you belong?' My parents heard that often when they first arrived. I might come from Orkney but I often didn't feel it was where I belonged. At primary school, 'English' was a term of abuse.

When I was little, the only black kid at the secondary

school went missing. He lived up near the cliffs of Yesnaby. His younger brother came on our primary-school bus and the adults talked seriously at the bus stops. A week or so later his body was found washed up at the beach. My playground experiences made me assume that racism had driven him to the cliff.

As an adolescent I didn't want to become part of what I saw as a subtle conspiracy to present Orkney as an island paradise. Tourist information proclaimed the beauty and history, endlessly reproducing pictures of the standing stones or the pretty winding street of Stromness when what I saw was boring buildings and grey skies. But although I regularly complained about Orkney, I was on the defence as soon as someone else was sceptical of its charms.

It's a push and a pull familiar to many young people from the islands. We ended up back here again and again, washed back, like the inevitable tide. I grew up in the sky, with an immense sense of space, yet limited by the confines of the island and the farm. On a day off from cleaning, the wind was in my hair down at the harbour in Kirkwall, which smelt of fish and diesel; out to sea, lights twinkled on the low hills of the north islands, Shapinsay, Sanday, and beyond them, over the horizon, Papa Westray. I was conspicuous and discontent in that small town after having lived away.

When we were teenagers we mocked the tourists. This World Heritage Site was our home, not just somewhere holidaymakers could buy tickets to see. After hours, when the coach tours had left, my brother, friends and I climbed into the stone Neolithic houses and tombs, with fingerless gloves and disposable cameras. In the morning the attendant would find burned-out tea-lights and empty wine bottles.

I was a physically brave and foolhardy child. I climbed up stone dykes and onto shed roofs. I threw my body from high rafters onto hay or wool bags below. Later I plunged myself into parties – alcohol, drugs, relationships, sex – wanting to taste the extremes, not worrying about the consequences, always seeking sensation and raging against those who warned me away from the edge. My life was rough and windy and tangled.

Growing up in the wind leaves you strong, sloped and adept at seeking shelter. I was far away when the farmhouse was sold, the value of the farm and our home split between my parents. Dad kept the farm and installed a caravan there for the nights he wasn't staying with his girlfriend, while Mum bought a house in town and rarely visited the farm again.

Mum was a farmer's wife and a farmer's daughter but also a farmer herself. As well as doing all the cooking and housework for the family, she drove tractors, mucked out cattle, built fences and dykes, and filled in the potholes in the farm track again and again. She and Dad worked together to dose the sheep with wormer and clip the feet of the ones with foot-rot, and to pick the stones, which each year worked their way up from the earth's mantle, from the ploughed fields before the barley was sown. Dad sheared the sheep, then Mum rolled the fleeces into tight bundles. After the divorce, she missed the farm terribly but it was too hard to visit.

★　★　★

Every cleaner was female and every room that we cleaned was occupied by a man. These women cleaned and scrubbed and washed all day at work, then went home and did the same for their husbands and children, and had done for years. They were experts. As I watched my supervisor's finesse with the mop, how she squeezed at just the right pressure and angle for optimum water and bubbles, I knew I would never achieve such skill. I thought that the firemen on the island were capable of doing their own laundry and changing their own beds.

As I paired up grizzled socks, threw away discarded pornography and cleaned toilets, I wondered if I would be happier if I had never left. Would it be easier if I'd married someone I'd gone to school with and stayed off the internet, if there had been less of a gap between my aspirations and reality? I thought about my mum. Maybe she had wanted more too. She was not much older than me when she found herself with two kids, abandoned on the day she gave birth and many times after that. She was a capable and caring woman, pushed to her limit on a cliffside farm on a strange island.

Mum turned to the Church when my brother and I were small and she was looking after a farm and toddlers while her husband was in a psychiatric ward two hundred miles away, across the sea. Once she had to sell the whole sheep flock because she couldn't manage them on her own and didn't know when Dad would be back. They thought that might be the end for the farm but they managed to piece it back together. In many ways, her faith kept the family going for a long time but, later, it was part of what broke it up.

Dad would say the modern, evangelical Church found her, preyed on and brainwashed her. She would say she was saved. It depends who I'm speaking to as to which side I agree with. I remember people from the Church helping out and decorating our living room while Dad was in hospital. He remembers coming back and finding new Bibles and religious books in the house, in their bedroom.

As the days grew shorter, it was dark when I left home to go to Flotta in the morning and when I returned at night. At the end of Orkney's long, bleak winter I was fading, hiding in the shadows. One afternoon, carrying my Hoover up a glass stairway, I walked into a shaft of sunlight. I looked around to see if it was safe, and lay down on the carpet, the light warming my hair.

Another day, when my supervisor found me crying in the toilets, not for the first time, she told me, with the kindest intentions, I had to leave: this was obviously not where I wanted to be. With my next wage slip, they sent me off on the workers' boat for the last time. A few days later, I walked into each room of the farmhouse, saying goodbye, before leaving with a rucksack and a one-way ticket for London.

4

LONDON FIELDS

M AY IS MY POWERFUL MONTH of change and possibility: it's my birthday and my middle name. There is a manic freshness in the air: I cut my hair and take baths at six a.m., draw pictures, wear strange dresses, apply for jobs and take drugs. There are new people to fall in love with and I have a spark that attracts things, needing less sleep and food. I drink more. My body feels right and I walk straight and strong across town. On these days composed of quests for experience, I say yes and pull on my boots again, excited and uneasy.

We called it a picnic although no one was there for the food, of which there was little – a few tubs of corner-shop dips turning crisp in the sun and a punnet of cherry tomatoes. Our group was sitting around a rainbow-striped blanket. It was one of the first truly hot days of the year and the sun on my bare feet felt luxurious. I ran my hands up and down my legs under my long skirt.

In London, with our commutes and travel cards and high rents, we could be isolated and had to find new ways to make a community. Each weekend when the sun shone we went down to the park, to London Fields. There was an unspoken rule that all the kids who thought they were cool went to this bit of dirty grass near the pubs, off-licences and cash machines, while the families and dog walkers were over by the play-park.

This was where suburban-bedroom fashion-magazine daydreams could almost come true. Looking for my friends, with electronic music on my headphones, I walked past lolling groups of Gothic ballerinas and landlocked urban sailors on the grass. Each girl in the park had taken time to consider her outfit: fifties housewives in gingham dresses and headscarves, eighties aerobics teachers in leotards and leggings, aristocratic hippies. The boys looked like mods, skateboarders or underweight lumberjacks. It was hotter than it had ever been in Orkney. I was in a foreign country.

When I moved to London, I threw myself in. I arrived in a flurry, with no certainties apart from some sort of self-belief. Several nights a week I would get on the bus to the Soho and Shoreditch nightclubs that I'd read about in magazines. I would try out colouring in my fair eyebrows with red eyeliner or slashing the back of a dress with scissors, and go down to the bus stop with a bottle. I met a lot of people in that first year, characters I identified from online message-boards and introduced myself to while waiting for the band to come on. 'I'm a penniless newcomer, can I write for your blog?'; 'I've seen you on Friendster'; 'I've read your online column.'

It was a relief when the first person from our picnicking group suggested going to buy booze. Banknotes were thrust towards them with requests for cider and wine. The rest of us waited, the girls making daisy chains and plaiting each other's hair, and the boys taking turns on someone's bike. We were overgrown children, not men and women, searching headlong for a good time. Text messages invited more people to join us, the next party, promising something better or more. Each weekend was more messed up than the last. We were careering around, taking taxis and buying drinks we couldn't afford.

Next to us a circle of wide-eyed club kids, who hadn't slept the night before, one in a lion's headdress, were taking photos of each other and laughing.

Our conversation was about work opportunities, whether the internship might result in some paid work, name-dropping fashion designers, magazine houses or record labels. Someone dressed in leggings, like an eighteenth-century lord, was complaining loudly about how the budget for his project was only ten thousand pounds. I heard a girl asking around for LSD, and it felt like the perpetual last day of a festival. A guy on a phone said, 'Someone could make a killing here.'

As the afternoon turned into evening, we moved with the sun until all the groups of people were crowded onto one corner of grass covered with cigarette butts and empty cans. Nearby, men drinking cans of strong lager from thin blue plastic bags were selling odd selections of books and ornaments laid out on the footpath: a pink plastic telephone and a book about fondue cookery, a pair of children's rollerskates and a kettle with no lid. You could get a bag of weed if you asked the right person.

It was Gloria's birthday and someone had a bottle of poppers. We were dismissive, recalling teenage headaches, but passed it around, sniffing between swigs from bottles of pink fizzy wine.

Meg was wearing tiny shorts, a halter-neck top and Lolita sunglasses, and had one foot hooked around her boyfriend's thigh, although her body was pointing away. Someone in a full suit too hot for the weather came up and asked if he could take her picture. 'It's for a street-style website.' She gave an exasperated look, then complied, posing expertly.

A group of parents and pushchairs walked by, an alien species, and Meg said to act normal. 'But I don't want to be normal,' said Gloria. She was wearing a bright turquoise jumpsuit. Meg smeared the honey we were using to mix sickly cocktails over her slender ankle, above her cork wedge shoes, and ants began to crawl onto her. We tipsily watched the tiny animals rush to their sugary doom as Gloria blew bubbles from a bottle. Someone said it was cruel but Meg insisted the insects were having fun. She was so beautiful and I wanted to shake her.

The trips to the off-licence grew more frequent, the shrieks louder, and the poppers were passed around. Someone, it might have been me, dropped the bottle and the contents spilled onto the rainbow blanket. We all dashed to the wet spot, heads down, gasping in the fabric, snorting and squealing, like pigs at the trough, breasts down, ankles up. It was stupid and pitiable and fun, as I breathed in the solvent, rolled onto my back and looked at the sky. As the horizon tipped I was covered with warm light and flying with my friends, limbs and sun cream and honey and ants, all sticky and sweet, and the sun was blinding me, and I had never been so high.

The sun lowered. The crowd gathered and tightened; flexed ankles met listless wrists and hands holding cigarettes. There were shaded glances down on the grass and drunken daydreams somewhere up there where the aeroplane vapour trails crossed. My bare toe touched his weekend stubble. I notice his bruised shoulder and felt my pulsing ambition.

Later, at the warehouse party, I'd lost the others but I didn't mind being alone. Hair twisted high and tight, in my long dress, with my drink and the drum beat, I was so far above. I was becoming more and more myself, white shoulders and red mouth flashing through the crowd, a plume of smoke hand-flicked and rising.

I saw the occasional familiar face and liked the feeling of knowing people. Everyone there had something that they 'did' – making music, running a nightclub, designing clothes – but was not yet making a living from it. We all thought we would be running things in five years.

A gang of art-school graduates, nearing thirty, lived in that converted warehouse, sleeping in garden sheds and using the rest of the high-ceilinged space to make music videos and experimental films. Over pre-disco drinks, they were competitively critical. Clubs were over soon after they opened but when they closed down were remembered with glowing nostalgia. Finding fault marked refined taste and superior experience.

The warehouse was used as a 'cool-party' location for films, making the landlord feel he could raise the rent, forcing the inhabitants out, meaning it was no longer the place for cool parties. This was a party to celebrate moving out. There were so many celebrations. A visitor from Scandinavia wondered just where he had found himself and why the hell everyone was drinking so much. 'You can't be dancing all the time,' he said, and I didn't understand.

Then I was out on the pavement alone, walking – with my jacket hooked over my arm and a bottle of beer – enjoying the night air on my bare skin. I was wasted but I wanted more. I wanted to rub the city onto my skin; I wanted to inhale the streets. I was walking faster, in worn-down boots, than the buses were travelling. The drugs I'd swallowed earlier made my breath fast and my cheeks tingle. Biting my mouth, I wanted to eat it all. There was heat in my face and lips and nipples and clitoris. I flicked open my cigarette box and went in again with the flash of the lighter and the quenching mouthful of drink. I could feel it entering, breathing deeply so the bubbles of oxygen processed the alcohol more quickly, sucking the smoke and holding my breath, squeezing each moment.

I had been walking through the city for so long that I didn't know where I was. I'd walk towards any light, towards the highest point. I wanted to reach up above the buildings, following the part of me that needed cliffs, and the air to be clearer.

★　　★　　★

When I made it home I lay on my bed with the window open. There was some wine left and I listened to sad songs and looked at uninhabited Orkney islands on Wikipedia. The night air was still warm, my hair was smoky and my skin dirty. I could hear bins crashing – the late-night takeaway packing up – and drunk people getting off buses.

Outside the flat there were raised train tracks and a smoggy crossroads. When cars with powerful speakers stopped at the red lights, the whole building vibrated in time with the bass. Although the sea was a hundred miles away, and some kids in the area had never seen it, there were seagulls hustling around. I once saw one carrying a segment of Terry's Chocolate Orange.

My bedroom, at the back of the house, overlooked the beer garden of one of the most notorious pubs in Hackney, which gained its fame by being open late at night after the clubs had closed, sheltering gangsters and alcoholics. Its reputation made it popular with the new waves of twenty-somethings who had moved into the area, into flats – ex-council, above shops – which, first, the Cockney families had left and now some of the Bengalis, too, looking for better things further east where London turns into Essex.

That night the pub held its weekly karaoke, the full-hearted, badly tuned versions of 'Mustang Sally' and 'My Way' infesting my sleep. Some were doing it mockingly, some seriously, but they were all so drunk that the difference did not matter. The wails drifted up into my room and mixed with the laughter and arguments from the beer garden, which lacked any soil or plant life and offered only ashtrays and umbrellas advertising lager.

The sky blended downwards from black to blue to orange. The neighbours' fridge must have been broken: they were storing their tonic water and meat on the windowsill. The new offices across the road were fully lit, yet empty. A factory, with a chimney of forgotten purpose, now housed art students, turning out their bedroom lamps and closing their laptops – one hundred wireless networks password protected, one thousand humans in an acre holding their wallets close to their genitals.

In the morning I could tell what time it was by the traffic noise. I could hear the call to prayer from the mosque. When my alarm clock rang for a few seconds I was rootless, without body or mind, but I didn't panic in those moments before realisation.

The residents of my rented flat kept changing and it was hard to remember who was living there and what jobs they had, if any. Lately, there seemed to be more people around in the daytime, and envelopes from Hackney Revenues & Benefits Service were pushed through the letterbox along with the unpaid bills. London is where you come to meet your match. People who were the coolest at their provincial disco or the cleverest in their school class are out-styled and outsmarted. Given a few titbits, like an internship or a good party weekend, they decide to make the move. We chose uncertainty and overcrowding with a possibility of success and excitement.

One flatmate was a musician who worked in a bar and, on the rare times I bumped into him in the kitchen, shared morsels of good news, like an email from a potential manager, but it was hard to tell the fairy godmothers from the sharks. The goddess on the dance-floor in a Cleopatra wig and a bikini put on her glasses the next morning and sat in Reception at an insurance company, browsing the internet. A stripper ran a techno club on her night off. I was temping in the parking department of a borough council on the other side of the city, writing record reviews on documents hidden under my spreadsheets.

The Afghan shopkeeper downstairs was the only person who had anywhere near an idea how much I drank. As evenings and months progressed, my trips grew more frequent into the shop where the light through the window was blocked out by fluorescent stars advertising special offers. Outside the door of the flat, the same man asked me for money, or a cigarette, or a cuddle, each day: 'Love, love, spare us some change, love.' The next day his eyes were swimming and he did not recognise me.

Back in Orkney, my friend Helga had told me that there is a mysterious, vanishing island called Hether Blether to the west of the island of Rousay. Although some Orcadians claim to have seen it, no one has ever been there.

The legend goes that a girl disappeared from Rousay and, after some time, was given up for dead. Years later, the girl's father and brother were out fishing when their boat was enveloped in a cloud. They came ashore on a strange and beautiful island and were met by the girl, now a woman, who told them that this was Hether Blether and she was now married to a man from the island and there she had made her home. She gave them a wooden stake and said this would allow them to reach the island again but the stake fell overboard on the trip back to Rousay.

There are many versions of the story and different Orkney myths of imaginary or vanishing islands – the magical Hildaland is linked to what we now know as Eynhallow – as well as similar stories from other places, often associated with foggy sea conditions. In Orkney, banks of sea mist appear and disappear quickly, perhaps the story's origin.

Vanishing islands still occur. Last year, geologists in the south Pacific on an Australian surveyor ship undertook a journey in which they were able to prove that an island shown on maps, including Google's, did not actually exist. Sandy Island is now defined on Wikipedia as a 'non-island'. It has been undiscovered. Cartographers say the phantom island could 'turn up' nearby – the Coral Sea area is vast and remote – having been wrongly located by mistake, or it might never have existed at all, created as a joke or as a test to expose cartological plagiarists.

There are islands of seaweed, islands of plastic and islands of sewage and other human waste. After volcanic explosions, rafts of pumice that look like islands can drift across the oceans for decades. There are islands of seabirds, puffins sheltering together in the months they spend out on the winter seas without ever coming to land.

Hether Blether is still enchanted, rising only on rare occasions. Some say that it is only visible on leap years. Anyone who sees the island should row towards it while holding steel in their hand, always keeping their eyes on its shores. If you are able to set foot on Hether Blether, you will free the island from its spell and it will become visible to human eyes.

When I left Orkney on the ferry it was foggy; arriving on mainland Britain was like emerging into another realm. I'd crossed a boundary not just of sea but also of imagination. Because I came from an island, London was the fantasy and London Fields was my Hether Blether. I became accustomed to an unsustainable enchanted lifestyle of summer days in the park with beautiful people and intoxicated nights at parties. I didn't expect the spell to be broken and I didn't want to find my way back through the mist to home.

5

NIGHTBIKE

THE FIRST TIME HE SAW me I was climbing on top of a phone box. We were outside a gig held in an empty shop on Kingsland Road where a rap group from south London took to the middle of the floor and the crowd circled around them. In the audience a model was pouting in a duck costume and I noticed a boyish American with mischievous eyes. Later, I sat on the pavement and told passers-by I was going to the beach. I could feel the tremors.

Although we didn't talk that night, I found out afterwards that he'd written about me online. He was worried about me but found me interesting. I was intrigued so the next weekend I turned up at a club where I knew he would be. I went up to say hello, touched him gently on the arm, and saw my reflection in the expanding black pupils of his eyes – dark floods of desire. When he spoke, my skin was alert.

We left together in a taxi for a house party where we'd heard a French DJ duo were playing. We sat on the doorstep and kissed, totally easy. When my friends went home I told them it was okay to leave me with him. The sole fell off my boot as we walked back to my flat. I don't remember much of that night but I do remember the night we spent together the next weekend, and the ten nights in a row after that, when there were electrical storms and we watched the thunder and lightning over London from his bedroom window.

The lightning over skyscrapers in the City was different from at home on the farm where it flashed over the sea and was followed sometimes by power cuts and phone lines going down. There were once reports, during thunderstorms, of ball lightning – St Elmo's Fire – inside houses on the West Mainland.

I sought connection with a fired-up fury, the secrets in his pupils, laughing his name with my legs around him. Each time made my heart beat faster and I'd cycle to work smiling in the morning through Dalston and Hackney. We texted all day until we rushed to meet again.

When we walked together he took me down unexpected routes and side streets. In the morning, sometimes, he looked like a hedgehog waking from hibernation. He was sensitive to hot and cold and many other sensations – cycling down windy streets and cooling his feet outside the duvet. We told each other about where we came from. He talked about his work technically and precisely and was different from most hipsters in Hackney because he had a proper job. He had an escape route.

In those first weeks, I stopped in the pub on the way over to his house and, over a couple of pints, wrote him a letter about how I was scared alcohol would come between us. Although we chatted easily about the small things, there were the gaps when I wasn't there. I'd drink until my eyes went dead. Back then he had patience for my tears and blank-outs.

We were in a bubble. At two a.m. one night, in his bedroom in Dalston, I said I was so happy I would never forget that moment. We hadn't met each other's families when we moved in together after six months: a one-bedroom flat above a book-maker on Hackney Road.

There were many more weekends and evenings after work in the park, with more and more people turning up. We felt at the centre of things. There was a gold rush of cool to this area of London, everyone afraid of missing out. After I met him I took him along too, showing off our partnership to the group. I look back at photos from that time and we're holding each other too tight, every limb and finger entwined, not looking at the camera.

I said I was never going back to Orkney. I ignored phone calls and letters. The farmhouse was being sold and I didn't want to know. My brother had moved away, too, following me to university. I was as angry with Mum and her faith as I was with Dad and his girlfriend – the woman he'd had an affair with several years earlier. But sometimes a smell in the air would remind me sharply that I was living in England. This leafy country with its red-brick skylines was not my home. I yearned for the open skies and grey stone of Orkney. I missed the curlews and oyster-catchers, even the black-backed gulls. Sometimes I'd be walking down Bethnal Green Road, surprised by the tears rolling silently down my face.

On the island I was big. It was secure and unquestioned but all I wanted to do was leave. Now I'd prised myself into the city, with its constant life and content, and there was no one else to blame. In London it was not possible to look everyone in the face but I wanted to touch everything. I was all eyes. It felt impossible to make any sort of impression on a place so big but I was going to.

I hadn't been particularly young when I started drinking, fifteen or sixteen, at teenage parties and dances in the auction mart. They were held in the room where the cattle were penned before sales. I loved seeing my friends and classmates – lumpen and self-conscious at school – open up, their inhibitions breaking down. Somehow I was often the one who took our half-bottle of vodka away on my own. I wanted to drink, fuck and photograph everything, but I'd end up in horrible states, crying, lashing out, my parents called. I wanted to experience things and no discipline was going to stop me.

With teenage friends in Orkney, I swallowed dried magic mushrooms we picked from the fields and walked around the harbour town through the graveyard. I tried to bite or kiss the cathedral, my mouth on one of its red-stone pillars, then drove twenty miles back to the farm, stopping for lights on the road that weren't there. I got home and scrawled in my notebook, urgently recording the fading sensations.

When I first left home the level of my drinking was not unusual for a student; the hangovers weren't so bad. In the same way that Guide camp or school activities seemed tame to farm kids used to climbing on roofs and scrambling down geos, the Students' Union was not enough. I found druggy clubs and outdoor raves, often accompanied by my brother. I balanced weekends taking 'party drugs' with weekdays reading and writing essays, often finishing them over a bottle of wine. But every year it got worse. As people around me began to drink and party less, I drank more and partied alone.

In London, months went by when I didn't leave Zones One and Two. Years went by in a blur of waiting for the weekend, or for my article to be published, or for the hangover to end. The drinking took hold of me. While others worked, turning down a night in the pub to reach the next London rung, I was emptying cans while on the phone, hiding the sound of the ring pull, talking of ambitions unfulfilled.

A photograph caught me unawares. He said I often looked like that: unfathomably, unquenchably sad.

On another unfamiliar bus route to a new temp job, I wondered if I'd ever feel at home again or if I would be blinking under a new light for ever. I wandered day-long, carrying phrases. At night I pushed my feet against the wall and felt as if my body was falling. There were flashes of happiness, a wild, open joy of life in little things that pleased and enfolded me. I felt lucky but could never hold on to it. Another Sunday muffled and hung-over in bed, makeup oily in my eyes, doors slamming somewhere, while up north the waves still curled dark and endless, and the aurora lit up the sky.

Sometimes, around two or three a.m., when I had not drunk enough to sleep, I crept out of our flat. Without turning on the lights, I carried my bicycle down the narrow stairwell, felt my way along the walls and slipped out into the street. After central heating and the close stench of bodies, the night air was refreshing. It was cool and clear, like my mind.

I never felt sad when I was on my bicycle. I used no lights, wore no helmet and knew the location of every twenty-four-hour garage and off-licence in a five-mile radius – fluorescent oases in the shut-down city.

Poised at the lights, my foot hovered above the pedal, ready to unlock the down stroke of energy that meant I was off, gliding round the corner, into the breeze. Breaking off Hackney Road, lurching into Bethnal Green – just me, the lonely taxis and night buses. I startled a cat into running over wet concrete, leaving paw prints for ever.

The canal opened the city up. It was the lowest I'd ever seen it, and among the usual cans and plastic bags, there were a digital camera, a saw, citrus fruit and a BMX. I pedalled faster, insects and branches ricocheting off my limbs. A swollen dead fox was floating in the black water.

On my birthday in May, with multi-coloured helium balloons tied to my saddle and a bunch of flowers in my basket, I cycled the straight stretch from my office across London Bridge, through the City and Shoreditch, then along Hackney Road to our flat to tell him I had lost my job. It was warm in the rush-hour smog and van drivers shouted and beeped, but at night I travelled swiftly and smoothly.

As I cycled I tried not to think about the lost jobs and all the disappointments. The air was getting warmer. Delivery vans were bringing tomorrow's newspapers and plastic-bagged bread. All the lights were green and a handsome boy in a top hat was sobering up at a bus stop. The police helicopter above was not looking for me. I tried to breathe in the dawn and realised I missed the sky.

Pedalling on, I chased the sensation of escape. I felt like I had as a teenager one night at the farm when the full moon was shining on the sea so temptingly that I left the house and walked down to the beach. I didn't need a torch: I was guided by the moon reflecting on the puddles in the road. The tide was high and the sea was swelling in the bay. I sheltered from the wind behind a sand dune and looked up at the perfect whole moon, its light catching on the waves, forming a shining path out across the sea. Looking back towards the farm, the dark island was illuminated by just the moon and the only other lights were stars, the glowing windows of cosy houses and my lighter, which briefly flamed, then the red tip of my cigarette. On the way back up to the farm, flying geese were silhouetted against moonlit cloud.

★ ★ ★

One warm night, crazy and hopeful, I tried to reach Hampstead Heath for sunrise. On the towpath, I pedalled too fast and, swerving to go under a bridge, tilted uncontrollably and felt the crash of my cheek on the water, the weight of my bike pushing me down. I was submerged in the canal for seconds in slow motion before surfacing and dragging my sodden body to the bank where I lay flapping, like a fish, my right shoe lost under the dark water.

I pulled my bike out, then my diary and squeezed the canal from its pages. Pushing my bike with one shoe on, I came home to him bleeding and crying. It wouldn't be long until he couldn't take it any more.

6

FLITTING

I HEARD IT SAID THAT IN London you're always looking for
either a job, a house or a lover. I did not realise how easily
and how fast I could lose all three.

I woke up crying. It was 1 May and I should have been
hopeful and happy but something in the night, some dark unease,
had crept into the room and into my dreams. Although I'd been
warned it was coming, I hadn't known it would be today. Without
telling me, he had taken the day off to pack up his stuff, separ-
ating his plates, papers and clothes from mine, untangling two
years of intermingled lives. When I got home from work all that
was left was my belongings, with dusty spaces where his had
been.

When he was gone, I spent a week alone in the flat, making
it through days in the office blankly. I'd been told I was losing
my job and was working out my notice period. Our bedroom
was destroyed – violently rearranged furniture, lines of poetry

on the walls, books and photos on the floor. I couldn't afford to live there alone.

I threw an apple against the wall and it lay rotting on the floor until the day he came round to clean for the new people who would be moving in. He told me that would be the last time and afterwards, using Sellotape, I collected his chest hairs, which had gathered in the sweat in my navel, and stuck them in the pages of my diary.

He had an escape route and he took it. He'd never meant to get so tangled with the wild girl on the phone box. I'd caught around him, like tights in the laundry.

When we met we were both drunk, then we drank together but at some point we no longer did. We didn't have wine with meals. He wouldn't touch me when I'd been drinking. He'd get home from work late and I was on the floor. He tried to take the glass from my hand and pour the rest of the bottle down the sink but I cried and said I hadn't done anything wrong. I was allowed to drink, I said. He drank when he went out with his friends. I drank myself apart – from him and from everyone. I undid myself. I tried to pretend the bottle was the first when I knew he'd heard me go out to the shop for more.

The eye contact dwindled. I squeezed the last love from him.

That May was, I felt at the time, the worst month of my life: shaking in the office surrounded by powerless colleagues, smoking nine cigarettes in my lunch hour, developing an aggressive obsession with my mobile phone, going on a shopping spree for smaller-sized clothes – yellow skinny jeans from Dalston shopping centre – getting my eyelashes tinted in a salon and having an allergic reaction. I had four job interviews and four rejections.

I remember swigging expensive vodka from the bottle in a suite at a fashionable hotel before falling asleep at a bus stop, climbing over fences and being dragged angrily around a polished floor by my ankles in a silk party dress, trying to go to an AA meeting but ending up in a 'spirituality workshop', surrounded by middle-aged ladies in long skirts with bells sewn to the hems.

I spent eight days in southern Spain, with Mum, unsuccessfully trying to get the sun to bleach my mind, writing pages of distress in my diary in red biro, drinking one-euro beers, watching the Eurovision Song Contest in an Andalusian bar, convinced I was having a proper conversation even though I couldn't speak Spanish.

Trying to make an afternoon pass by spending my dole money on an unsustainable pose of iced coffees and political magazines, I had a dish of Turkish stew delivered to my solitary table where, with papers, diary and phone spread out, I looked like someone with things to do. At the next table six silent women were munching joylessly through fried breakfasts. They were all wearing bunny ears.

I scanned the internet blank-eyed for a solution that was not forthcoming, I cycled round east London aimlessly, with a bag full of confusion. I was drinking more than I was eating.

*　　*　　*

In Orcadian, 'flitting' means 'moving house'. I can hear it spoken with a tinge of disapproval or pity: the air-headed English couple who couldn't settle, the family who had to 'do a flit' quickly due to money problems. In London I was always flitting but was too battered to see it as an opportunity. I wanted to flit quickly so that no one noticed, slipping from one shadow to the next.

I boxed up my things and moved them to a storage unit, then went to stay with my brother, who was living with his girlfriend in Dalston. He helped me move my belongings but he didn't know how to help with my bottomless pain and increasingly out-of-control behaviour.

Tom is twenty months younger than I, and as toddlers we were zipped into jackets and shod in wellies, and rode in the tractor cab together. As children, we made dens at the top of the hay barns, above the bales in the eaves, where it smelt sweet and dusty, and mice would dart out. We played in the barley store, the grain like quicksand. In summer we swam in the rock pools with friends, the water always bracingly cold. We reared caddy lambs with bottles before they were put back with the main flock – always a bit different, smaller and misshapen.

In the rafters of the big shed, raised from the ground, there is a hut made from half caravan, half wheelhouse-from-a-fishing-boat, and from there we would jump onto woolsacks at shearing time, soft and oily. When we were teenagers I often shouted at him to get out of my room but sometimes we rode the horses along the Bay of Skaill, galloping across the sand and in the sea as tourists at Skara Brae took our picture. I could never do impersonations but he could and I'd ask him to perform Orcadian characters: our grumpy primary-school bus driver, who swerved to hit rabbits and in his spare time ran an abattoir; the dinner lady who called out, 'Plenty o' seconds!'; the man who read the mart report on Radio Orkney.

Tom followed me to university, where we went to raves together and then to London, where we had many of the same friends. Later, he watched me drunkenly posting on the internet and answered when I phoned, distressed, late at night. It was Tom who came and got me from the hospital the night I was attacked by a stranger.

Sleeping on Tom's sofa was a temporary arrangement. I knew I had to find somewhere to live, and looked at adverts online for flatshares. The adverts described households as 'chilled' or 'creative', perhaps euphemisms for their choice of drugs. Sitting in the park with a bottle, or in an internet café with a can, I called the numbers numbly, gave basic details about myself and arranged times to visit. I marked the addresses in my *A–Z* with a green felt tip, forming a dot-to-dot of my search on pages 68-9, Hackney and Tower Hamlets.

I looked at around twenty rooms, groups of people – friends or strangers – who wanted to be in London enough to pay the high rents and live in flats where five unrelated people shared a kitchen. Some were proud to tell me they had a sitting room, even when it could barely fit a sofa. A warehouse was split into apartments and the small room I was shown had a bed raised on a platform and no windows. I imagined shutting myself in there with books and whisky and said I'd take it. They chose someone else.

In a Haggerston tower block where most of the windows were either broken or boarded up, I went to see a room on a Saturday afternoon. The curtains were drawn, loud trance music was playing and the place smelt of cannabis. I said I'd let them know. In Homerton two girls, both said they were actresses, were just moving into a large, bright apartment, their handsome boyfriends carrying their boxes of clothes and antique furniture up the stairs. They gave me peppermint tea and asked why I was looking for somewhere to live. I mumbled my story. They chose someone else.

One sunny evening I cycled to see a room in Clapton, then the cheapest area in Hackney, where terraces of dark-windowed houses lined the last hill before the Olympics site. The residents were friends-of-friends and younger than me, born in the nineties. It was a small room in a Victorian terrace, and when I saw the sash window next to the bed I knew I'd be able to drink and smoke freely there. A few days later I moved in.

I was struggling to understand how I'd let myself lose another job. I'd seen it coming, documented in depth the reasons why it was coming but repeated the actions that would make it come. Then it had come. I wasn't in control.

I thought I had it sorted out: a job in an obscure corner of the publishing industry, where the days were hung-over, the deadlines relaxed, and I came in with a different nightclub stamp on my hand each morning. I wrote complimentary profiles of corporate leaders, keeping my head down, arriving late and leaving on time, weekends messing it up, then ghostlike working weeks trying to piece it back together.

And then I was unemployed again, blinking away tears as I left another temping agency, wondering how far the money I had would get me in this unforgiving city. I was a tourist, useless and homesick. I craved horizons and the sound of the sea but when I walked to Tower Bridge again London took my breath away.

No one held their head that high in the Job Centre, even the boys who had cars waiting for them outside blasting hip hop, or the man dressed in a suit, ready for work, or the woman waiting next to me who smelt so sour I had to cover my nose and mouth with my sleeve.

I didn't get replies from most of the jobs I applied for. Sometimes I felt there were just too many people in the city. I felt unwanted, like I'd failed to find my space. My friends were now spread over different areas and groups or I'd lost touch when I moved in with my boyfriend. I was no longer at the centre of things.

I got an interview in the tallest building in the UK and was pleased that I'd never had vertigo. I bought a beer after the interview and looked up at the tower block: it reminded me of a cliff face and in particular St John's Head on Hoy – the tallest cliffs in the UK, which I used to see from the ferry to Scotland. It was always windy at Canary Wharf, the breeze off the Thames funnelled between the tall buildings, which made me feel at home. Peregrine falcons nest on cliffs and tower blocks, and as night came, the aircraft warning lights on tower tops were like lighthouses on the islands.

Although I'd left, and had wanted to leave, Orkney and the cliffs held me, and when I was away I always had, somewhere inside, a quietly vibrating sense of loss and disturbance. I carried within myself the furious seas, limitless skies and confidence with heights. I remembered sitting on my favourite stone, looking out to the Stack o' Roo, watching seabirds from above. The colony of Arctic terns on the Outrun had dwindled and disappeared but more gannets were appearing out to sea. Hardy sea pinks grew at the cliff edge and I used to see white tails disappearing down rabbit holes where puffins nested. The ledge felt solid but, looking from another direction, you could see that it was overhanging. Unsettled in London, I felt as if I was dangerously suspended high above crashing waves.

I usually started drinking as soon as I got home from work. Sometimes I got off the bus halfway and had a couple of cans in the park. I couldn't wait, and when I was unemployed I didn't have to.

Drunk, I spilled an ashtray and hoovered a still-lit cigarette without realising; the smell of burning dust, skin cells and hair in the bag hung around the flat for weeks.

There was something in the attic that creaked and scratched and had, we thought, been causing the unseasonal volume of flies. The landlord eventually sent someone around to have a look. There was a hole in the roof where pigeons had been getting in and becoming trapped. In the space above our sitting room, just above our heads, a pile of dead pigeons was rotting.

That summer I felt as if I was just passing time, not living. I was in a blank-minded, waiting-to-feel-normal state for months, flitting from one thought to another. The weather was warm and I had itchy palms and sweaty thighs. I got up in the night and smoked cigarettes at four o'clock after lonely, empty days.

A distant car alarm kept me awake until dawn, until I could no longer distinguish its incessant chatter from birdsong. It was a balmy July night in London but in those hours I imagined myself in every bed I'd ever slept in and even wondered at what hour he would crash in from a nightclub. I had the sensation that I was experiencing everything I had ever done or felt at the same time. I remembered how we had slept on the roof of the art school once, among concrete blocks and discarded sculptures. I remembered the thunder and lightning every night of the first week we spent together and that room without curtains where in bed we watched planes crossing London and created a new language.

In the morning I remembered, with a lurch. My bassline had dropped out. When he'd left me I'd gasped and hadn't exhaled.

7

WRECKED

One January afternoon, my brother's tenth birthday, we were playing in the farmhouse when the phone rang. Something had happened on the Outrun.

Mum, Dad, Tom and I went outside, through the farmyard and out of the gate towards the shore, meeting neighbours heading the same way. We fell into nervous silence as our pace quickened. When we reached the edge of the cliff, she rose into view: down below, a large fishing boat was balancing on a sloping outcrop of rock. With each incoming wave the vessel rocked, unsure whether to be washed back out to sea or be pushed the other way, into the cliffs.

It was only mid-afternoon but it was getting dark and the tide was rising. The next wave came and there was a sickening creak, followed by a thunderous crash. The boat had tipped the wrong way and her hull had cracked. She was stuck. No tug boat would be able to pull her off the rocks now.

It seemed like a disaster for our cliffside group but we were joined by a coastguard; he told us the fishermen who'd been aboard were not so concerned. Hours earlier, under cover of darkness, the crew had climbed over the edge of the boat, dropped down onto the rocks, picked their way along to the lower part of the cliffs and scrambled to the top. Instead of knocking on the door of a farm, they'd gone to the airport and had left Orkney on the first plane.

Udal Law, the Norse system that still applies in some cases in Orkney and Shetland, has different rules about the ownership of the coastline from the rest of Britain. In other places, owner-ship of land extends only to the high-water mark but in Orkney it extends further out to the tide's lowest spring ebb. Other interpretations of the Udal limit of land rights include: as far as a stone can be thrown, a horse can be waded or a salmon net thrown. Under this law, if something comes ashore on someone's foreshore, it becomes their property.

The next day, the farmers knew they had to take their chance and climbed down the rocks the same way the fishermen had come up. I watched Dad go first, long-legged, clambering aboard the boat, then helping others up. We held our breath, hoping their weight would not tip the vessel, before watching them disappear inside the cabin. They emerged a few minutes later and, although they were too far away to see properly, I could tell that they were beaming, arms full of computer equipment.

Over the next few days, with the farm work continuing, one of our byres became a showroom of electronic navigation and fishing equipment, and fishermen from all over Orkney came to look and buy. The farmers made a deal to give the insurance company five hundred pounds so that they could sell everything from the boat, including the catch; the profit came to many times that.

A few days later the wind got up and the boat was toppled from its perch. Overnight, the force of the sea against the rocks smashed it, leaving only small pieces floating on the waves and washed up in geos.

Almost twenty years later, like the boat, I was in a precarious position. The division between my appearance-maintaining daytime reality and the secrets of my nights was slipping. The cracks were showing. The worry about keeping my cover left my back aching and my hands fidgeting, rolling cigarettes. I was in a dangerous loop, now consciously drinking to ease the shame of what I'd done while drinking the night before.

The things I did in shared flats were usually not so much bad or dramatic as stupid and annoying: making a mess when trying to cook drunk late at night; eating flatmates' food as I never had enough of my own; their alcohol drunk and replaced, drunk and replaced; asking to borrow ten or twenty pounds to see me over until payday, then going to the off-licence, slipping back into my room with the door closed and the window open.

I would put a token number of bottles and cans in the recycling, then tie up the rest in carrier bags and push them into dustbins on the street. I left the house chinking and smelling of stale booze.

There were empty bottles in the bottom of my wardrobe and empty cans lined up along my bedroom skirting board.

My behaviour brought tension into the household: unpredictable noise levels; Tuesday-night parties with strangers, men I brought home; leaving my handbag outside the front door and possessions trailing up the stairs. These episodes were followed by the depressive shadow of my hung-over days in bed.

I was always getting into horrible states but what other people perhaps didn't realise was that I didn't want to get into horrible states. I remember and respect the people who had the courage to try to talk to me about my drinking. I would nod and cry but after the break-up I was self-pitying and self-justifying. 'You're quite right to be worried about me,' I'd say. 'I'm in pain.' He'd left me because of my drinking so now I was free to drink.

It wasn't the break-up that tipped my drinking out of control, although I used it as an excuse. While I was still living with my boyfriend, I went to a friend's birthday party in a bar in central London. I left after an hour or so and a couple of drinks, saying I was tired or ill or going home to write when in fact I was going home to drink alone at a faster pace than the drinks were coming there. That evening I chose alcohol over friends and had crossed a line. After this, I crossed lines quicker and quicker, choosing to drink despite warnings from work, doctors, family and the law.

I wished there was a reset button on my emotions, history and compulsions so I could forget about what I had lost as I lay awake listening to shrieks and bass from the street below. I made plans to be out there, getting it back, jolting emails from daybreak, getting fit, having a radical haircut and typing the words that would save me, but it didn't happen and I kept ending up in the same place.

Half cut in bed I wanted to speak to him and whispered out loud, 'I am shining a light over the city for you. Stay warm, keep safe, wherever you are.'

Everyone began to know that I was trouble. I didn't get invited to so many parties. I was a burden, the girl who always cried. I knew I was in trouble after that Saturday. I hadn't thrown the bottle at the girl's head although that was what it had looked like to everyone in the pub whose eyes turned at the crash and scream. Instead I threw the bottle down towards the table and it ricocheted upwards to hit the innocent, now-screaming girl. I realised the differentiation did not matter.

There were many times I recognised I had a problem and resolved to change. I went to some AA meetings. On a concrete step outside a church after a meeting in Holborn, drinking a milkshake, watching Boris Bikes pass me, I had an unexpected feeling of calm but that weekend I was in a mess again, drinking from two p.m. until two a.m., climbing over walls. To show my distress one night I stripped naked in a stranger's flat.

Over the course of a month I was involved in events that meant I appeared in court twice, first as a criminal, second as a victim. I'd only ever been into a courtroom as a newspaper reporter before.

Referred by a doctor, I started going to a counsellor on Friday afternoons; she made me write a 'drink diary' and I promised to limit my intake. Later that day I was in the off-licence, buying just two cans but going back half an hour later for more. It was never just two cans although I told myself, on hundreds of occasions, it would be. I spent my nights drinking alone in my bedroom, increasingly few people inclined to talk to me, in another undistinguished job. I thought, now I was single, it would be a good time to 'have dinner parties' and 'take my portfolio to editors' but I found myself crying in doctors' surgeries, waking lower and lower each morning with more mysterious bruises.

Part of me enjoyed the wildness of running across London, alone on the top deck of a bus with a can of lager, but it was rarely fun at the end of the night, drooling and lonely. I never gave myself up completely – I always tried to function at work, eat well, stay social and afloat – but it was a painful and exhausting cycle, trying to maintain a hold on balance, always trying desperately to smooth my rough edges.

In another new house, a flat in an ex-council block in Tower Hamlets, my flatmates began to understand that I was drinking alone in my room, then coming out in wildly different moods, and confronted me about it. I got a by-now-familiar 'We need to talk' email, followed by the sickening drop in my stomach. I'd let people down before and couldn't bear to fuck up again. Broke and borrowing money to buy booze or convincing the local shopkeeper to give me some cans on tick, I avoided bumping into my flatmates and neighbours in the corridor because I knew they could hear me crying at night.

It was not the outer chaos – the problems with other people

and money, the lost and broken possessions – that was the worst thing. The worst thing was the state inside my head. The suicidal feelings were increasing in frequency and strength. I was not in control of my emotions. My thoughts and behaviour were swirling and unstoppable. He doesn't love me any more. I miss him. I don't know what to do with myself. I can't see how I can go forward or how I can get over this. 'You have to tackle the alcohol problem,' they said, but how could I when I felt like that? I felt like a sheep stuck on its back: I knew I'd suffocate but it was easier just to stay lying in the hollow.

Months passed: a winter, a disastrous trip to Orkney, where I spent time in a police cell, another under-employed summer. I couldn't believe the sadness had gone on for so long. The searing panic was something beyond me and I ignored all rules and safety measures to follow it, a slave to the habit of pain. Eyes always brimming with tears, I had fortnight-long headaches, bad dreams I couldn't wake from. I had gone beyond and didn't know how to get back. I saw the pattern from the curtains of my farmhouse bedroom. I could feel the tremors, and the wind of memory was flowing through me too fast to hang on.

Everything had been speeding up during the years I had been in London until I was out of control. The city required me to filter so much out – faces, advertisements, events, poverty – and my mind had been making the filter ever tighter until all that I was left with was whirring space. I was dumbfounded and unable to make decisions about where to go, whom to see or what opinion to hold, filling the void with alcohol and anxiety.

And I cried that I was adrift, helpless to the irrational need, the desire. I was falling, swirling, trying to find a point to hold on to, but as I grasped, any target moved further away.

I was running out of options. Although there was lower I could fall – more trouble, further to be cast out – for me, this was enough. One night I had a moment, just a glimpse but it was expansive and ambitious, as if the blinkers were temporarily lifted and my view was flooded with the light, when I saw a sober life could be not only possible but full of hope, dazzling. I held on to that vision and told myself this was my last chance. If I didn't change, there was nowhere else for me to go but into more pain.

8

TREATMENT

O N MY BELLY ON THE floor, back arched, arms stretched behind, fingers locked, I was trying to hold my breath. The teacher, attempting to put us in touch with our primal selves, said, 'You were born to do this,' and my pose collapsed in laughter with everyone else.

Had all my life been leading up to doing Kundalini yoga with a bunch of pissheads and junkies in various states of physical disrepair and mental anguish on an institutional carpet? A particularly difficult move had to be repeated thirty times but the teacher promised, 'By the end you'll be flying.' Addicts all, we chased that high.

In the catalogue of my hangovers it was not spectacular but one morning a month or so earlier I'd decided to accept whatever help was on offer to deal once and for all with my dipsomania. I was running late for work, desperately trying to claw myself together, dehydrated and panicky, as I was on so many mornings, but that day my will just broke. I couldn't do it any more. I remembered the sensation of the night I'd been struck by the dazzling glimpse of possible sobriety. I called my boss from the bus and said I needed to talk.

It had taken a long time to get there and to accept that this was my situation. When I was younger, it was not my plan to be in rehab when I turned thirty. The fact that I'd only just realised life did not work out how you expect or want showed I had been lucky until then.

I'd been reading some old diaries. Just before I'd left Orkney at eighteen, I'd written an arrogant list of all the things I wanted to achieve but also, perceptively: 'This world of art/fashion/ literature/rock and roll that so attracts me could be my downfall.' A decade later I'd had a lot of fun and had a lot of stories but had also, year by year, day by day, developed a damaging compulsion alongside dissatisfaction and loneliness.

For years, I had occasional insight into my problems but was somehow unable to take the action I needed to deal with them. Drunk, I'd talk fluently about my drinking problem. The day after a dreadful binge, I would resolve again and again to make a fresh start.

I made three serious attempts to stop drinking and managed about one month each time: once, in a failed attempt to stop my boyfriend leaving me; once, trying to keep my job, on Antabuse medication that provokes an allergic response to alcohol (didn't work); and the previous summer, in a failed attempt to prevent my flatmates kicking me out. This time, I'd lost the boyfriend, the flat and the job and was faced with the reality of doing it for myself, which is really the only way. This time I decided to put sobriety first. I quit my new job, saw my doctor and was referred to the council's drugs and alcohol advisory service.

It wasn't the out-of-the-way location, the tatty seats or the blank bureaucratic dealings that made me sob while I was in the waiting room at the addiction clinic: it was the smell. It was the same sour odour that had filled my London bedrooms, the smell from an ill sheep you are going to have to spray with a red X and send to the mart. Not the same as the smell of booze, it is a sickly fragrance emitted from the pores of a creature whose internal organs, liver and kidneys, are struggling to process toxins and push the poison out though the skin, fingernails and eyeballs.

I remembered that acetone smell from when I was a child and sheep lay dying. One morning Dad went into a field and found more than twenty ewes on their sides or backs, blown up like balloons, others stumbling around as if they were drunk. They had been put into a new field the night before and gorged on chickweed in the grass. Fungal blooms in the plants had produced froth, causing them to bloat and stopped them burping. Gases were building inside them and their tubes were blocked. In a desperate attempt to save them, Mum and Dad moved between the stricken animals, pouring vegetable oil into the throats of some to break down the froth, and plunging spiked tubes directly into the stomachs of others to release the gases. Tom and I watched in horror as they worked. Many sheep were saved but five died in the field and a couple more over the next few days.

★　　★　　★

I asked to be referred to a residential rehab – I wanted to be locked up – but instead the advisory service decided that as I was classified somewhere between a dependent and a harmful drinker it would be more suitable, and cheaper, for me to go to a 'day programme' and remain living at home, which was by this point a single bedsit above a pub in Hackney Wick. I drank heavily in the fortnight leading up to starting the programme – my last chance – and called my doubtful family while half cut to explain my plans. When I told Dad I was doing this for three months, he was sympathetic and said, 'I've spent three years of my life in psychiatric care. I hope it's less for you.'

After a week of 'community detox', in which I went each day to the centre and was given sedative Librium to help with any withdrawal symptoms, a breathalyser test and more tablets to take at home, I started the twelve-week programme. It was, and still is, 100 per cent local-authority-funded, staffed by full-time counsellors and admits up to twenty clients. When I joined, it had, despite a very high drop-out rate, produced more than a hundred 'graduates' – people completing the twelve weeks while remaining abstinent from all drugs and alcohol – since 2006.

The first day at the treatment centre was strange. I had to give a urine test, with the toilet door open. It didn't take long to undo my shyness as we had to pass a piss and breathalyser test twice a week. There was no coffee allowed in the centre, and although I went home alone every night and cycled in every morning, for the first two weeks I had to be accompanied if I left the building at lunchtime in case I decided the group therapy and handholding were just too much and ran off to the pub or coffee shop.

Out of the group of ten who were there when I started, only one or two others and I were there 'simply' for alcohol; the rest were also addicted to cocaine, heroin, crack or other drugs. They included older Cockneys, who genuinely used rhyming slang, and Muslim rude boys who spoke in patois I didn't understand (phrases like 'raggle fraggle'). But people were often not as they seemed at first. I'd noticed a little plaster on someone's inner ear and all week I'd thought it was some sort of 'gang thing', until they explained that it was from the previous week's acupuncture session.

We attended Monday, Tuesday, Thursday and Friday from nine thirty until four thirty. Apart from a weekly one-on-one counselling session, our days were spent as an intense group. The four daily sessions included group therapy, weekly updates of our 'clean time', talks on things like nutrition or blood-borne viruses, and workshops on topics like 'relapse prevention' and 'self-esteem'.

Wednesday was our day off, when we were expected to have doctors' appointments, sort out benefits, see probation officers, and otherwise unpick the messes that addicts tend to create. As part of the programme, we had to attend three AA or NA meetings a week outside the centre.

On my first afternoon we had a session with a brilliant nun who was in her seventies and had worked with addicts and in prisons for years. At one point she misplaced her red marker pen, even though it was right in front of her, and one of the 'old timers' (he'd been there about six weeks) whispered to me,

'She's pissed.' This is a well-worn joke in rehab but it made me giggle and giggle.

We stood in a circle and held hands at least four times a day, reciting the 'Serenity Prayer', which, despite its strangeness at first and my distaste for religion, I soon began to enjoy. But I was shocked. I was often confused and upset about how I'd ended up there. I was a girl on a farm on an island and I'd woken up to find it was twelve years later and for some reason I was in a rehabilitation centre in London, or sitting in Salvation Army centres and church halls with groups of misfits, drinking tea from chipped mugs, listening to tales of people shitting the bed as we laughed our heads off.

We had written work, based on AA's 12 Steps, which we read out to the group. We went into detail about our pasts and I shared dark and shameful things I had never told anyone else – we all did and it created trust and a bond between us unlike anything I'd experienced before. Unlike drunken confidences and late-night conversations, I could remember these the next day.

I worked hard, trying to answer honestly the questions the counsellors asked me and making an effort to listen to the others. I wanted to be the star pupil of rehab. The act of writing those lists of the unwanted effects of my drinking made it clear to me that I did have a problem and I was in the right place.

The decision to choose abstinence seemed extreme to me but I had found, through painful experience, that my attempts to control and limit my drinking always failed. Once I started I was unable to stop. AA's basic principle is not to take the 'first drink', after which the alcoholic is 'powerless', and to keep doing this 'one day at a time'. The theory says I lived – and continue to live – with two things: the obsession and the craving. The obsession shows itself in the desire to drink, which pulses through me unexpectedly, like the tremors at the farm, an almost imperceptible rumbling that is always there, threatening, in the background. It will, I think, remain with me for the rest of my life. I need to stay vigilant and not have the first drink that triggers the craving – my inability to stop. If I let one trickle through, I'll be flooded very quickly.

When we drink, alcohol, or more specifically ethanol, is absorbed into the stomach lining and enters the bloodstream. In the brain, alcohol confuses messages between neurotransmitters and acts as an intoxicant and a depressant or relaxant. For those of us susceptible to addiction, alcohol quickly becomes the default way of alleviating anxiety and dealing with stressful situations. Through repeated use of the drug, our neural pathways are scored so deeply they will never be repaired. I will always be vulnerable to relapse and other kinds of addiction.

All day we were encouraged by the counsellors to voice our 'feelings' about everything we said or that happened in the group. Addicts' emotional responses have been warped and suppressed by substances and it was important for us to regain an understanding of our state of mind and what those feelings made us do. Pressed to find a 'feeling' to express about some drug-induced criminal activity, one of my 'peers' (as we called each other) reached deep within himself and came up with 'ride it like a soldier'. While this was not strictly a 'feeling' it made us laugh, releasing the tension in the room caused by repetition of 'ashamed' and 'sad', and became a catchphrase in the group.

Funny, revealing things happened every day. One lunchtime we were talking about vitamin supplements (most of us alchies had been prescribed various types of B vitamin), how useful they were, whether it is better to get vitamins through eating fruit and vegetables. 'I mean, when you've had a salad, can you immediately feel it doing you good?' I realised that, because we were all addicts, the conversation had quickly developed into how much of a buzz you could get off a carrot.

Another day, two uniformed police officers turned up at the centre and immediately most of the guys – I was the only woman for some time – were sweating and reaching for their coats. It turned out they were on a routine visit, not looking for an individual, but it gave me more of an idea about my new friends.

One morning a peer turned up wearing a Jack Daniel's T-shirt and was told not to wear it again. He hadn't realised that it might be inappropriate. I told him – a recovering junkie – that I'd wear my heroin T-shirt the next day.

But there were reasons why we needed to be vigilant. Somehow a pint glass got into the kitchen cupboard, with Red Stripe (one of my old drinks of choice) branding, and we were soon discussing our favourite types of beer: real ales in huge glasses or super-strength cans of lager. It was enough to get the cravings going. In the treatment centre, saying, 'Cheers,' instead of 'Thanks,' was risky territory.

A couple of times we got to leave the centre: a visit to the City Farm and to an NA convention. It felt like a combination of a school trip and a prison break: a collection of giggling raggle fraggles set free on the London public-transport system without our keepers. I would never have joined a group like that elsewhere and, alongside the pain of quitting drink, I had moments of genuine joy. At the City Farm the sight of a former crackhead sitting calmly on a rock coaxing three lambs to join him made us all smile, and another of my addict chums showed me how the fourth knuckle on his right fist was flattened from, years before, punching a cow. I noticed that the lambs were scruffier and the fields barer than at home in Orkney and pushed away some unwanted fond thoughts of home.

Some days my thoughts wouldn't stop and I just wanted to escape myself. I began the habit that I've continued of drinking masses of Coca-Cola, which, alongside cigarettes, hit some approximation of the spot. I wanted to eat my own teeth, crunched down with Coke, until I was sick. I wanted to be put into a medically induced coma. I wanted the future now. I wanted to care for other people and not live on my own any more. I wanted nothing more than to stay sober but I wanted a fucking drink.

Back in my bedsit in the evenings after the treatment centre, I was exhausted. I was trying to be honest with myself for the first time in years. I didn't drink, although I often wanted to, and lay on my bed with the internet and the window open. On those summer nights I couldn't believe winter existed. In the same way, when I tried to imagine Orkney, it was nothing but Dreamland.

After 'class' one day, I went to visit a couple of guys who had left the treatment programme (one finished the twelve weeks, the other was asked to leave after eight) and were now in the supported housing block where they lived with twenty or so other male addicts. It was a strange place: the en-suite rooms, secure entry system and smell of stale smoke made it feel somewhere between a hotel, prison and student halls-of-residence.

Said was the same age as me and, despite the differences between us, his life over the last decade had been a similar catalogue of broken relationships and lost jobs. He'd smoked crack and heroin for years but, when I visited, it was five weeks since he had finished the programme and he had been clean for more than four months.

He told me how he had left school early after getting into trouble for fights and vandalism, then selling drugs. He'd made many attempts to get clean, including being prescribed methadone and spending time in Bangladesh, but always relapsed. This time, he said, he wasn't running away from his problems. After his last use of heroin in February, he had been in detox for twenty-one days before joining our treatment group. Said's success was the exception rather than the rule. The treatment programme were unable to give me statistics, but of the ten people who were there when I started, only two successfully graduated. One left after she decided it was too intense, one was asked to leave for 'failing to engage with the programme', and five were discharged (kicked out) because they relapsed (they drank or took drugs).

More people joined when I was there, with a similar relapse rate. The programme was tough. Although it had the same 100 per cent abstinence and zero-tolerance policy as a residential centre, each night and weekend we were sent back into the real world, with its pressure and temptations.

While I was visiting Said, a man who had been discharged from the programme in my second week, following a relapse, came into the kitchen. The deterioration in his appearance was shocking. He had lost weight and teeth, and his hands and face were covered with sores, which the others later told me were cigarette burns. He told me that, after leaving, he had gone on a bender culminating in a five-day stay in the psychiatric ward of Mile End Hospital. He said he was back in AA meetings, trying to stay off the drink and feeling 'better', but his wild eyes told a different story.

At seventy-three days since I had had a drink, more than two months into the programme, one of the main 'feelings' I had was a sense of luckiness. I listened all day to the others' stories and was so sad at the places their addiction had taken them. In group therapy one day, one of the older peers was talking about his family, from whom he had been estranged for more than a decade due to his chronic drunkenness. He said he had learned not to think about them too much, and when he went to sleep, he told himself that he should not dream about them, son, daughter or wife. 'But then I have no one to dream of.'

Another peer, in his fifties, a former heroin user and dealer, was reading out his homework in which he talked about his childhood love of sailing, fishing and 'open seas', and his once-tender relationship with the wife who had divorced him in the eighties. Everyone in the circle, including the counsellors who had heard so much already, and men who had spent almost half their life in jail, was fighting back tears at wasted lives, thwarted ambitions and broken hearts.

I had never injected drugs, been a prostitute, smoked crack in front of my baby, spent eight years in a Russian prison, mugged an old man in the park, or been through six detoxes and four rehabs, painfully relapsing each time. My family still spoke to me and I had not turned yellow. I looked around the room and realised that everyone who had been married was either divorced or separated. I was glad I had stopped when I did. I didn't want to break anyone else's heart with my drinking.

I also felt lucky that I'd had the luxury of taking three months out of the 'real world' to sort my life out, publicly funded, with the support of the excellent counsellors on the programme. With the coalition government making cuts to the public sector, the future for resource-heavy programmes such as this one was unclear. The prime minister was talking tough, picking out addicts and people with weight problems (there were apparently around

80,000 addicts on incapacity benefits, including 42,360 alcoholics – my peers were surprised at how low this number was), saying that the public only wanted to pay taxes 'for people incapacitated through no fault of their own'.

I thought about drinking all the time. It was there at the back of my mind, like tinnitus, with regular intense cravings shooting through my mind and body. And then there were the dreams, the drinking dreams. I dropped a bottle of wine on kitchen tiles and was lapping the drink like a dog, along with dirt from the floor and broken glass. I woke so relieved that it wasn't real.

One afternoon we had acupuncture, awkwardly handling our imaginary glowing balls of *chi*, needles sticking out of our ears and third eyes, trying to take the pan-pipes music seriously. I rushed, all anti-Zen, for a cigarette, then to hoover the room (we had different 'therapeutic duties' each week), before jumping on my bike to power along the canal to a bench I'd found. Lightheaded, with sweet blossom swirling in the breeze around me, waving at mysterious officials in orange boats, an ice-cream van Yankee Doodling from an unknown location and aeroplane trails across east London's sky, I thought, This is wild. I was finding that being sober could be kind of a trip and I was just riding it like a soldier.

9

DRIFTING

A T MY BEDSIT IN HACKNEY Wick, six single people lived above the pub, on one floor divided by the landlord into the smallest individual living spaces possible so that he could squeeze the most rent from the building. The rooms were separated by thin walls but I heard very little noise from the other occupants, no conversation or laughter, just TVs. There was a shared washing-machine in the hallway but I never saw anyone else using it. We all waited until the hall was clear before scuttling into our rooms or out of the door. Migrant workers, divorcees or alcoholics, no one planning to be in that situation for very long, six lonely people so close but transient and unable to reach out to each other.

I had chosen to be there because it was the cheapest place in east London I could find to live alone. I could not risk relying on or letting down other people again. My attempts at sobriety in the past had failed and I wasn't confident enough to count on this one. I was just taking things day by day, sitting on the end of my bed, my possessions crammed around me, smoking out of the window, looking across the canal to the newly built Olympic stadium, anxious and frustrated.

I'd left my job to go to rehab, so when my three months in the treatment centre came to an end, I found myself unemployed again. I was treating my sobriety with great care, as if I was a delicate, newly hatched chick and I was not going to let myself be shaken or squashed. I was trying to pay attention to my needs and emotions, anxious, tired, lonely, hungry, which previously I'd usually dealt with by an unsubtle and ultimately unhelpful application of booze. I was going to AA meetings and avoiding some old places and people, while applying for jobs with a new hard-to-explain gap in my CV.

I drifted around east London on my bike, hoping that by acting as if going swimming, buying groceries, texting people from AA and drinking endless Coca-Cola was enough, then it'd gradually become so. Alcohol had been my companion for years and, although it had caused me trouble, I was missing it.

When I broke up with my boyfriend I'd spent a long time feeling it was almost futile to cook for one. What was the point of watching a film alone, or of sweeping the floor when it was only me walking on it? I still missed him – I thought of him every time a plane flew over east London – but he was gradually getting further away. I was now going through something similar with alcohol. What was the point of picnics without booze? Was I supposed to just meet a friend, not 'for a drink'?

Aimless, jittery and jonesing, any small thing going wrong

upset me disproportionately and I was spun out. The workings of the city and my mind had been exposed, and things made even less sense than they had when they were concealed. Layers of complexity multiplied and I couldn't hang on. I cycled around the roundabout under Canary Wharf, where there were trade entrances to the shining office blocks above, Chinese waiters smoked and I breathed in trapped traffic fumes. I cycled through Hackney Wick, where on one side of the road a storage facility was packed with people's possessions and on the other there was a newly built empty apartment block.

I was coming around to the idea that alcoholism is a form of mental illness, rather than just a habit or lack of control. Although I knew that everything good happening in my life – regaining the trust of my family, who'd seen me promise and fail to change many times, possibilities of new work, a slight confident step – was reliant on me staying sober, as I cycled over the bridge across the Eastway in the sun, knowing I had a free afternoon, I had the thought that a couple of beers would not only be a nice idea but was the only thing that would give me satisfaction. Although I didn't think I was crazy in general, thoughts like that were insane. I had to stay vigilant.

I kept thinking about a Bloody Mary, which I'd rarely drunk. A Bloody Mary with plenty of vodka through a straw sitting outside a bar by myself. When I was craving, I would abandon all else and just drink into oblivion. But I was learning that the thing with cravings is that they pass: I sat through it and an hour later wondered what it had been about.

In a strangely landscaped park in the middle of Canary Wharf, under the shadow of Number One Canada Square, I drank an overpriced coffee, watching men in suits and women in wrap dresses and heels talk on phones, security passes around their necks. Just a few months earlier, I had worn smart clothes and was buzzed into corporate headquarters but now I felt removed. I was in an ill-fitting, garish dress with messy hair, shaky and tearful. I'd given it up voluntarily, and was glad I had, but there were moments when I wondered what the hell I'd done.

As well as stopping drinking, my time in rehab changed me in other ways, reconfiguring my priorities. I felt lucky to have indulged in treatment and to have met all those loopy and unpredictable people. Working with people who could barely read and write, but who often expressed themselves with eloquence that hurt my heart, made my concerns over things like grammar seem petty and obscure. Hearing about life in prisons, in hospitals, in travelling communities, in large families, in Russia and in Stepney Green showed me spheres of experience orbiting far away from media-saturated graduates bitching on Twitter. My old friends now seemed different, going round the same bars and parties, with the same topics of conversation. Excuse me while I smash up the drum kit inside my head.

I never cried when I was on my bike and, to get out of the house, I took long cycles across the city, through my past. I cycled along Regent's Canal, past the place where I'd fallen in. I stopped at the spot in Trafalgar Square where I'd left a bag full of new clothes and make-up after a shopping trip had turned into a solitary pub crawl. I cycled through Soho, where I passed familiar doorways to clubs and all-night bars, and down Brick Lane where, each year, a new influx of dressed-up twenty-two-year-old girls walked in groups of three.

Standing up on the pedals, with my hair blowing in my face, I felt like I had when I was a kid – uncool and undefended. The fresh air, the wind, was where I came from and, although there were buildings all around, the open landscapes of Orkney were still inside me and I was somehow always cycling towards a hidden horizon.

It was autumn but there were still some warm days, and when I passed the corner of London Fields where all the posing cool kids hung out, I got a flash of what they call in AA 'euphoric recall'. I had to fight to remember that the good times there, the impromptu picnics, only really happened in the first couple of years. Later, it tended to be just me, some cans of Kronenbourg, my notebook and a mobile phone I began to hate for not ringing.

The devilish thoughts flickered. I worried that my life was over and I'd never have fun again. I thought that if I wasn't going to amount to anything I might as well drink. I wanted to have a glass of champagne on a pavement outside an art-gallery opening with good-looking fashionable people, maybe one of whom would take me home if we got drunk enough. I wanted cocaine. I missed the moment where inhibitions gave way, and my heart ached for that brief enlivement. I had purposefully put barriers between myself and alcohol but was finding it hard to be restrained.

I parked my bike and sat on a bench by the canal, drinking a cold bottle of water, reading, in *Moby-Dick*, about bursting a whale's heart. Two lads with dreadlocks and long shorts were setting up a tightrope between two trees near the railway bridge. They called to me, asking if I wanted a go, so I ran over and slipped off my shoes. 'You could hold onto the tree or me, but the best thing to do is to use the power from your own push-up to balance yourself,' he told me. My legs quivered uncontrollably sending vibrations along the rope and, as Central Line trains thundered above, I tried to keep my back straight and my eyes on the horizon. I fell almost immediately.

Back in my bedsit, on Friday and Saturday nights, I'd tensely smoke out of the window, listening to the pub downstairs, wondering if this was all there was to sobriety. I felt as if I had got myself ready for something but didn't know what it was. I was fit, healthy, clean, and home alone again all weekend, too scared to go anywhere. If this was the future, I didn't want it.

Coming out of rehab was not the end of the story but the beginning. Getting sober is one thing – I did it hundreds of times – but staying sober is a daily challenge in which there are moments when it comes together and I felt certain I'd done the right thing, then times when it was painfully hard.

It hadn't mattered to me so much when I was drinking but now I was feeling the distance between me and my family eight hundred miles away. I was speaking to my parents more. Dad needed some help on the farm and Mum encouraged me to come up for a visit. Although it was nearly winter, a short time in the island air while I was applying for jobs might help me regain my strength and appetite.

London wasn't the same. I was a stranger in my old life and

was discontent. But, back in Orkney, people had been to visit Dad on the farm, surveyors and businessmen, and there was talk of money. If the farm was sold, what would be there for me? What was next? What was the point of saving my life?

I plotted. I agreed with Mum that some space would do me good but part of me, the addict, had other ideas. Going back to Orkney would be a test. If I got to a year sober, still hadn't found decent work and still felt frustrated, I would get an anonymous job somewhere, maybe as a cleaner, move into another rented room, cut myself off and just drink. It would feel so good to give in.

10

DYKING

THE SKY GETS BIGGER AS the train travels further north. The temperature changes in inverse correlation, and for each leg of the journey – London, Edinburgh, Aberdeen, Orkney – I put on another layer of clothing.

I posted the keys to my bedsit through the letterbox of the pub, dragged my suitcase onto the bus and got to King's Cross early in the morning. I'm not settled until the train pulls away from the station and we are in motion. Although I've got good at negotiating the booking websites to find the cheapest fares, the journey is expensive and will take a whole day. I could have flown to any European capital in a shorter time and for less money. I sleep a lot on the train, waking every half-hour to pins and needles and new geography. Other passengers get off at their destinations – Peterborough, Durham, Newcastle – but I keep going north. Somewhere after Berwick upon Tweed, there's a rush of light into the carriage as the sky and sea open up. I'm in Scotland but not even halfway home.

After Edinburgh, we cross the Forth Rail Bridge and pass through Dundee. Getting the shorter ferry crossing from John O'Groats to Orkney would have meant staying overnight so today I get off the train in Aberdeen and don't have long to get from the station to the pier. Huge oil-industry ships are docked in the harbour and seagulls are hustling around. I'm rushing and crumpled, struggling with my luggage, but the sea air and a cold breeze hit me. It's been a while since I've tasted the wind like this. There's a sign saying 'Northern Isles Ferries' but I know the way. I board the boat at five o'clock to sail into the North Sea as night falls.

On-board, the ferry from Aberdeen to Orkney is kitted out to look like a hotel but cannot disguise the reality of its daily trips through the temperamental North Sea and retains the whiff of sick. The carpets are patterned to disguise vomit stains and the chairs are chained to the floor to stop them tumbling across the room in rough seas. When the captain announces over the intercom there might be a 'bit of chop', I know enough about Orcadian understatement to refrain from eating and swallow a travel-sickness tablet. I'd been told that if I was feeling seasick, I should hold my gaze on the horizon but right now I want to sleep.

I can't tell if people are drunk or if it's just the motion of the waves. I bed down under my jacket on the sea-rocked floor and watch a mother and son have an argument in sign language. Voices carry over the lounge in the Orcadian accent

I have not heard in months; it brings back schoolmates and neighbours. It's a Celtic lilt, vastly different from something like Glaswegian, somewhere between Welsh and Scandinavian, coy and almost sarcastic. Hearing the accent does not give me comfort but a jolt of anxiety and old feelings of not fitting in. I am too big and too English, remembering the sense of being trapped on 'the Rock', as frustrated teenagers call Orkney.

I buy a copy of the *Orcadian* from the bar and am interested in reading local news but at the same time don't want to bump into anyone I know. I am tatty and defeated, with bad skin and nerves. I don't want to have to admit that I've come back – that I've failed. I wonder if it's possible to really come back once you've lived away for a while, or if it's called coming 'home' when you never belonged.

I've been sober for a few months but I feel like a fraud accepting praise when people say 'well done' because I want to drink and feel it's impossible that I won't again. Yet I don't drink, day after day. Perhaps this is just how it is, I think, this daily battle and my small, careful life is what the so-called miracle is.

On my last trip home I spent the entire seven-hour ferry journey in the bar and had to be helped off the boat by strangers. This time, I am able to stand out on deck as the ferry arrives into Kirkwall around midnight, feeling the salty wind on my face as the lights of the harbour grow closer in the night. When Mum meets me I see her relief.

In the car on the way to her house, I remember how, when Tom and I were small, Mum would reach back when she was driving and hold our ankles to reassure herself we were still there. Even now she does it sometimes.

Mum now lives in Kirkwall, Orkney's main town, in the large bungalow she bought after the sale of the farmhouse. She lets rooms to lodgers but tonight there is one free for me. Although the house contains furniture, pictures and crockery from the farmhouse, I have never lived there and it's not my home. When we get back, Mum makes me a cup of tea and we sit at the big wooden kitchen table that our family of four used to eat around at the farm.

Once a month, around full moon, Mum goes to the Bay of Skaill as a volunteer to help with the RSPB's beached-birds survey. She walks the high-tide line, looking for, identifying and counting dead birds. The findings give information about disease, food shortages or oil spills, although she doesn't usually find much, a good sign. A couple of days after I arrive back, I join her. As we walk, we look across the bay to the farm – this is the closest Mum goes, these days. We find one dead fulmar, one dead cormorant and one dead sheep.

Mum drives back to Kirkwall and I walk up along the coast to the farm from the beach and notice, as they taught me to in the treatment centre, my feelings about the place: the surge of affection as the buildings come into view. The people who live in the farmhouse are no longer my family but this is where I come from and it's special to me.

Dad is here, although most nights he stays with his girlfriend. I'm thinking about everything that has happened when I sit down by the freezer, then decide to walk up to the Outrun. In his caravan, Dad tells me about the tremors and we go together to feed the Highland cattle.

I stay at Mum's for a few weeks, sleeping a lot, looking at job websites, signing on the dole and attending a few AA meetings in Kirkwall. Mum gets the worst of me. She is supportive and good-natured but I'm irritable. In Orkney I revert to a surly teenager. I know she is pleased that I'm not drinking but I don't want to discuss it, as if this would be to admit I had made some wrong choices in the past or that she was right.

Soon after I arrive back, there are storms. Although life in the town is different from at the farm – there are trees in the garden and we're more sheltered – Mum's house is still noisy in the wind. The daylight hours are short and I often sleep into them. At Christmas, I take a trip to Manchester to visit my brother and his pregnant wife. Life is carrying on and I return to Orkney, knowing that I need to do more with myself than just not drinking.

In storms last month, conditions – including hurricane-force northerly winds and water-logged earth – were such that sections of drystone dyke made of huge grey slabs, which had stood through gales for 150 years, collapsed all over the farm.

The morning after one storm, I walk along the shore, looking for driftwood or treasure. I find one unusual piece of flotsam: a seal, on the other side of the fence from the sea, perhaps carried by a huge wave. A young straggler, blown off course.

I've washed up on this island again, nine months sober, worn down and scrubbed clean, like a pebble. I'm back home, at the end of a rough year, in the winds that shaped me and where the sea salt left me raw. I've got a fresh start but I'm not sure what to use it for, so I'm going to make myself useful, building walls in the short hours of daylight and staying in a caravan at night.

After fifty-four days when it rained each day, with only eight hours of sunshine in the whole of December, there were some magical days in January: dreamy sunsets reflected on calm sea. Mum drops me off at the farm with my bags and I feel pleased to have something useful to do. Dad has shown me in the past how to build drystone dykes. It's slow work. A dyke is actually two walls, built to be flat on the outer faces, joined at the top by large linking stones and filled in the middle with smaller loose ones. Although repairing a broken-down section is easier than building from nothing, it's not breezeblock mindlessness: I have constantly to visualise and discriminate. I select and estimate the odd-shaped stones for shape and size, forming a unique 3D jigsaw that has to last.

The stones are heavy and ancient, and modern technology seems flimsy. I carry a digital camera and a lump hammer. When I crouch behind the wall to smoke, I watch the sun's short journey across the southern sky, over the Bay of Skaill and the hills of Hoy before it falls below the Atlantic horizon and I can no longer see my stones. I start to think in decades and centuries rather than days and months. I think about the people who built the original dykes, when the farms employed many more workers, and I wonder if my part will stay standing for as long. I have flitted and drifted but I want my wall to be permanent.

In the fading light the farm is timeless and two huge horses appear, like time travellers, out of the mist. When I was a kid, there were the bones of working horses down by the shore, left where they were shot by farmers forced to replace them with tractors. In 'Horses', the Orcadian poet Edwin Muir imagined strange horses coming back to the landscape after a future apocalyptic event. These two Clydesdales graze Dad's cliff fields; like in the poem, they have returned.

When it's finally built, the last big 'coping stones' lifted on top to bind the two sides of the wall together, I lie on the dyke on my back and let my head hang over the end. Upside down, I view the sky as if I am looking down on it. It seems deep and wide rather than a two-dimensional arc, with cloud paths stretching out into the earth's atmosphere.

I'm learning to identify clouds, cloud-spotting in the same way that others bird-watch. The international cloud-classification system defines clouds by genera, species and variety, using Latin names. The high wispy clouds are called cirrus and the ones in the shape of a fish skeleton are called vertebratus. Stratus, the grey, featureless sheet of a cloud we often have at this time of year, is known as opacus or translucidus, depending on whether the sun is visible through it. One afternoon, I spot some rare lenticular cloud, formed by the wind into cigar shapes.

I become interested in a fairly recently discovered meteorological phenomenon: noctilucent cloud, literally 'night shining', the highest and one of the rarest types, drifting in the upper atmosphere. Unlike most cloud it is made of ice crystals rather than water droplets. It's usually invisible but just after sunset around midsummer, in 'deep twilight', the tilt of the earth allows it to catch the last light of the sun.

Sometimes known as 'space cloud', its first recorded observation was in 1885, two years after the eruption of Krakatoa. It could be that the ice crystals have formed around specks of dust – from volcanoes, meteors or space-shuttle exhausts. I like the idea of pollution creating something beautiful.

Despite the absurdity of classifying the ever-changing clouds, trying to define the sky like this opens up new ways of thinking to me: of the beauty of Orkney's highly changeable climate, of rain as simply the decay of a cloud.

Just as these islands seem impossible when I'm in London, friends online talking about Japanese restaurants, new bars and the tube at rush-hour now seem preposterous. My fingernails are dirty, my lips chapped from the wind.

I'm repairing these dykes at the same time as I'm putting myself back together. I am building my defences, and each time I don't take a drink when I feel like it, I am strengthening new pathways in my brain. I have to break the walls down a bit more before I can start to build them up again. I have to work with the stones I've got and can't spend too long worrying if I'm making the perfect wall. I just have to get on with placing stones.

One night in the caravan, the weather turns wild again. Although it is well weighted down, the thin walls tremble and the wind and hail are crashing against the windows. It's like being at sea.

I have drinking dreams. I'm so thirsty. Each night brings up flashes of locations I had forgotten: the floor of a train, somehow under a table of four strange men, not sure if I was being sick; a small town in Spain, late at night, knocking on random doors trying to find what I thought was a nightclub; in London, crying on a pavement underneath a cash machine, ringing on my ex's buzzer in the middle of the night, unwanted; waking with someone in my bed who hadn't been there when I'd passed out. I wish none of it had happened.

Half awake, I have a sensory flashback, as I often do when trying to sleep, of the night I was arrested when the car swerved and hit the grass verge. After I moved out of our flat, I had come back to Orkney for a few weeks, heartbroken, to try to find some calm but it wasn't there. The police picked me up as I was passing the road leading to the cliffs of Yesnaby, which had become known as a local suicide spot. They had been alerted that I had gone out in a car, leaving two empty wine bottles, known to be terribly unhappy. They were waiting for me at the end of that road but I wasn't going to drive down it. I was driving to the farm, crazed with sadness. All I wanted was to get home.

I was so drunk that I had to close one eye to see the lines in the middle of the road. At one point I hit the verge – a sickening clunk – but regained control of the car and straightened up. For some time I had felt as if I was turning over endless stones looking for a safe place but I couldn't find one. The drink offered the promise of ease but even that wasn't working. My body was rejecting it – I would be gagging but trying to force more down.

When I saw the blue lights I thought at first it was strange that an ice-cream van would be out in the countryside. When they got me – sadly, acceptingly – into the back of the police car, I said, 'I didn't want to hurt anyone else.'

Trying to sleep in the wind-rocked caravan, the muscle memory of the car hitting the verge keeps jolting through my mind and body. Dropping off to sleep, I'm jolted awake. My car keeps swerving off the road.

Despite everything that has happened – the drink-driving conviction, giving up my job to undergo the programme and sort out my alcohol problem, all the pain my drinking has caused me, all that I have lost and all that I stand to gain through quitting – the thought of and desire for a drink still comes through me regularly, like an electric shock: when I hear a good song, or the sun comes out, or I feel angry, or I want to phone someone and tell them something nice. Alcohol is woven into nearly every area of my life and it will take some time to untangle and develop new responses and strategies. It takes a while to build a strong wall.

I've lived in ten different houses in the last five years. My belongings are in friends' attics and garages in London – a physical manifestation of my unsettledness and split loyalties. I am scattered and never at home. I think about having a drink like you might fantasise about having an affair. I know I can't do it, but maybe if the conditions were perfect and nobody would find out, we could have a weekend together, my bottles and I.

Each evening when I take off my overalls and work gloves, I hide in the glow of my laptop and don't drink. I want to drink but I have hope that something inside me will change. I'm back under these decaying clouds and deep skies, living among the elements that made me. I want to see if these forces will weigh me down, like coping stones, and stop the jolting.

II

AMBERGRIS

A MILE OR SO UP THE coast from the farm, a whale corpse is decomposing in a geo and I scramble down the rocks to investigate. Colossal internal organs are scattered among the seaweed and driftwood, and the skin is spread, like a carpet, over the pebbles. Examining the carcass, I'm caught unaware by a wave and jump up on the nine-foot spine to escape but still get wellies full of sea water and rotting whale slime.

These days a beached whale is somewhere between a curiosity and a tragedy but not so long ago it was a bonanza. The meat was eaten, if fresh, the blubber made into oil for lamps, lubricants or used in the manufacture of soaps and other products, the whalebone in construction and for making corsets. You just had to know what you were looking for. These days, bird-watchers know that dead whales bring rare birds. While I'm examining the dead fin whale in the geo, white gulls, Iceland and Glaucous gulls, more usually found in the Arctic, are hanging around. They were blown in on a weather system but stay for days, feasting on the carcass.

In different ways, whales have been used by people in Orkney for millennia. A whalebone hammer was excavated from the five-thousand-year-old settlement at the Knap of Howar on Papa Westray. One theory about the coverings of the now roofless Neolithic houses at Skara Brae suggests that, in the absence of much wood, the inhabitants used whale ribs as rafters, stretching animal skins between them, perhaps turfed on top. Bones twice the height of a man made a warm home, like a heart inside a ribcage.

In the late eighteenth century, whaleships called at Orkney on their way to Arctic waters, to take on fresh provisions and skilled oarsmen. In *Moby-Dick*, Herman Melville's narrator, Ishmael, says: 'How it is, there is no telling, but Islanders seem to make the best whalemen. They were nearly all Islanders in the Pequod, Isolatoes too.'

On 14 March 1955, around the spring equinox when the winds are often strong and seas high, sixty-seven pilot whales were stranded at Point of Cott on Westray, beached when they followed each other hunting or in rough weather. I try to imagine this sight and the excitement on the island at the unexpected event. On 7 December in 1994, when whales were now seen in terms of conservation rather than hunting, eleven sperm whales were beached at Backaskaill Bay on Sanday, where, collapsing under their own weight, they died the next morning.

At the furthest north-west point of the Orkney mainland, near a tidal island called the Broch of Birsay and fishermen's cove

Skipi Geo, there is a local landmark, 'the whale bone': an upright of a rib and a cross-piece of part of a skull. It was set up about 130 years ago by local people after they'd used the other parts of a washed-up whale. It is well loved and over the years has been blown down and reinstated many times, now marking the turning point at the end of a dog walk. I see a photograph of the whale bone with the Northern Lights and the Milky Way in the background, a raw, grisly sculpture with yellow lichen growing on the eroded bones.

A few weeks ago, Dad was chatting to a beachcomber friend and asked him to name the best thing he could imagine finding on the shore. 'Ambergris,' he replied. Ambergris is a rare and highly valuable substance, produced in the stomachs of sperm whales, either vomited or excreted, and found floating on the sea or washed up on the shore. Dad's friend described the substance – waxy, between white and grey and amber – and Dad said, 'Oh, we've got some of that.' A lump of waxy material fitting the description has been in the tractor shed for decades, ever since my parents bought the farm more than thirty years ago.

We've been reading everything we can about ambergris. Melville writes that it is 'soft, waxy, and so highly fragrant and spicy, that it is largely used in perfumery, in pastilles, precious candles, hair-powders, and pomatum. The Turks use it in cooking, and also carry it to Mecca, for the same purpose that frankincense is carried to St. Peter's in Rome. Some wine merchants drop a few grains into claret, to flavour it.' On the internet, we wonder at parfumiers' descriptions, of a 'pheromone' with 'a transformative quality' that 'seduces particularly feminine noses, who instinctively recognise the odour that will attract males', read claims that it can 'cure Parkinson's', and watch eBay auctions where lumps have been selling for forty dollars a gram, not much less than gold.

When my parents moved to the farm before I was born, there were whale bones around the buildings. I remember, as a child, climbing up a dyke and standing on a massive vertebra that sat on top, part wall, part animal. The remains give us a link to these sea beasts and encourage the idea that our lump might be what we hope. It is now the size and shape of a large naan bread or a toilet seat, although Dad remembers that it has changed shape over the years – to fit a bucket it was put in, then flattening out gradually when tipped onto the byre floor. It's a piece of farmyard junk that could easily have been thrown on a bonfire or midden.

Our fortune – how much? Fifty thousand? A hundred? – might have been sitting on the floor of the shed all this time: the answer to our financial problems in a lump of whale puke! Ishmael again: 'Who would think, then, that such fine ladies and gentlemen should regale themselves with an essence found in the inglorious bowels of a sick whale!'

We have been performing experiments, melting and poking fragments of our treasure, looking for the cuttlefish beaks that are a sure sign of a whale's digestion. Insertion of a red-hot needle produces a satisfying puff of white smoke but while there is some kind of smell it's not quite the 'peculiar odour that is at once sweet, earthy, marine, and animalic' we've read about. We are also concerned that the dogs and rats on the farm have never tried to eat it. In the caravan, Dad and I joke that the blob we're experimenting on is worth hundreds of pounds but we can afford to waste it. Results, so far, are inconclusive.

I've been fighting to avoid falling into the depression that is apparently common in the first year of sobriety, missing some of the chaos and unpredictability of my old life. There are many things I am scared may happen by surrendering myself to sobriety but near the top of the list is *losing my edge*. By 'edge' I mean my cool, by which I mean my enlivening sense of discontent, and my youth, and sex – narrowed eyes and full lips – and enjoyment of testing the boundaries, of saying something uncomfortable and an excitement in the unexpected.

I don't want to become someone sanctimonious, who tuts at teenagers drinking alcopops; neither do I want to talk in therapy platitudes nor acquire the evangelical tone of voice I know from church preachers.

But the truth is, my edge was blunted some time ago. I'd hear a great song and think, This'll sound fantastic in a club or live, with other people, but by the time I'd got there – if, indeed, I'd got there at all after too many over-excited sharpeners at home – I'd been too trolleyed to take in, let alone enjoy or remember, the music or conversation. Where was my edge when I was physically ejected from a nightclub in front of loads of people I know, kicking and screaming against bouncers, for reasons I don't remember and have been too embarrassed to find out? It wasn't cool to be crying at parties to anyone who would listen about how my boyfriend had left me because of my drinking while swigging from a bottle of beer in one hand and a glass of wine in the other. It wasn't a good look to ruin my friend's poetry reading with coked-up incomprehensible heckles, or to be lying on the floor of a pub toilet, my friends too weary to do anything to move me.

Alcohol wasn't working for me any more. I remember being so drunk I was falling down, but feeling I'd barely scratched the surface, buying shots at the bar, never able to fill the emptiness. The exhausting and boring cycle of alcoholism would have continued. I could have been a sad, lonely drunk of forty, fifty, sixty years old. In the end, I was chasing a promise that never delivered and now I'm looking to the surprises of my natural surroundings to stir my imagination.

Uncertainty is hanging over the farm. Developers have visited, interested in the Outrun. At this lean time of year, before the lambs have been sold, the suggestion of large sums of money is attractive. As with the ambergris, we're seduced by the idea that the land might provide an unexpected fortune.

The next step is to send a small sample of our 'ambergris',

for testing and verification, to one of the perfume houses in France or traders in New Zealand. Perhaps we're stalling to keep the daydreams of multiplying bank accounts and new tractors alive, in the knowledge that if something seems too good to be true then it probably is. Soon, all we might have is a lump of worthless wax but for now it's a thing of wonder and riches, magic washed up by the sea, thanks to the dyspepsia of a whale.

At one time our farm contained a 'smithy', where a blacksmith would repair other farmers' tools, ploughs dragged by horses and, later, tractors. Dad sends a sample of our waxy lump to a Parisian perfume company and they eventually reply saying that it is probably a crude form of animal-bone wax or glue, not ambergris. It's disappointing but while the lump doesn't connect us to the sea, it does link us, with blacksmith's glue made from the melted bones and hoofs of horses, to the history of the farm.

12

ABANDONED ISLANDS

I T IS NOT UNTIL LATER that spring that I see my first living cetaceans – the name for whales, dolphins and porpoises. On a small Rigid Inflatable Boat, returning from the uninhabited island of Copinsay, we are suddenly among a pod of harbour porpoise. The captain cuts the engine and they surface intermittently, six or ten of them, close enough that we can hear them breathe. The Shetland name for porpoise is 'neesick', onomatopoeia of the sound they make as they breach. On the small boat, we are at their level and everyone aboard is transfixed, talking in whispers. I'd always known that the porpoise were out there but to see and be among them is more moving than I'd imagined, an unexpected bonus at the end of a magical twenty-four hours on the tiny island.

Around the north of Scotland lie many uninhabited islands, abandoned in the mid-twentieth century when the forces of depopulation reached such strength that the last residents could no longer cling on. People had lived for hundreds, if not thousands, of years on those islands but the struggle to maintain life, combined with the potential of better prospects elsewhere, brought the communities to an end. Usually there was a trickle of islanders moving away but in some cases, such as on St Kilda in the Outer Hebrides, the whole community was taken off at once. HMS *Harebell* sailed with the last residents of St Kilda in 1930.

Orkney's abandoned islands include Cava, Faray, Fara, Eynhallow, Swona and Copinsay. Now on these lonely isles, left to the elements, empty houses fall into disrepair and farmland is reverting to moor.

Eynhallow – associated with the stories of vanishing islands Hether Blether and Hildaland – is a 'holy island', with an important part in the history of Orkney and the Norse Orkneyinga Saga, which recounts the history of Viking kings and earls in the Northern Isles in the ninth and tenth centuries. The landowner moved all the crofters off the island in 1851 after an outbreak of typhoid. When the thatched roofs and wooden partitions of the houses were burned to control the disease, the structure of an ancient monastic settlement was revealed. The church had been used as a dwelling place for generations.

On Swona, the descendants of the cattle left by the last inhabitants in 1974 have gone feral, the young bulls fighting for dominance of the herd. Meanwhile, parties from environmental groups go out for days castrating wild cats on uninhabited islands, trying to control the feline population, descended from domestic cats, which preys on birds and their eggs. On Cava, two women,

Ida and Meg, were the only inhabitants from 1959 until the early nineties.

I had passed another abandoned isle, Stroma, which is not actually part of Orkney but Caithness, on the ferry from Orkney to Gill's Bay near John O'Groats, and was taken aback by the number of houses, all now unoccupied, on its east side alone. At its peak Stroma had a population of five hundred but, after a gradual decline, the last residents left in the sixties to work on the construction of the Dounreay nuclear-power station just over the water. The island still has much of the structure of a community – pier, church, school, lighthouse – relatively intact but with no one in year-round occupation.

Copinsay is a mile long and half a mile wide to the east of the Orkney archipelago. Its population reached a peak of twenty-five in 1931 but the last residents left for the Orkney Mainland in 1958. Spending more time in Orkney than I'd planned, I take the chance to explore its edges and travel to spend the night on Copinsay with seabird researchers Juliet and Yvan, who are going there to study the fulmar, shag, kittiwake and razorbill. The island is now an RSPB reserve, home in the summer to thousands of nesting seabirds. There are no scheduled ferries to it, of course, and we make the forty-minute journey on a small vessel with local boatman Sidney, leaving from a jetty outside his house on the East Mainland.

Sidney moors the boat at Copinsay's crumbling jetty, overlooked by a derelict farmhouse. In an upstairs bedroom I pitch my tent, deciding to sleep in there for warmth, rather than outside in the wind. The house is startlingly similar to the one

I grew up in, a late-nineteenth-century Orkney farmhouse built on the site of previous steadings. The history of people on the island stretches back to the Iron Age, and Copinsay was known to the Norsemen as Kolbeinsay – Kolbein's island – perhaps named after a Viking chief due to its command of wide ocean views.

The Groats were the last family on the island, and had thirteen children. Under the decaying stairs, I find coat pegs marked with their names: Bessie, Isobel, Alice, Eva, Ethel . . . There are still beds and other furniture in the house that the family left. One room was used as a school when a teacher was employed for the Groats and the children of the lighthouse keepers. The lighthouse, the only other dwelling on the island, was automated in 1990.

Exploring the uninhabited buildings, I imagine the children in the schoolroom and playing on the small sheltered beach in front of the farmhouse and feel sad that no one lives here any more, but it's clear what a raw existence it would have been. The island provides the minimum needed to survive: it is a wedge of rock, faced on the north-east side with high cliffs, exposed to the wind, the salt-lashed land only enough grazing for a few livestock. There was not enough to keep the children here and, with ageing parents, they all gradually left. A lot of people in Orkney are now descended from the Groats, and the tale of the Copinsay Brownie, an ugly yet helpful sea beastie, has gone down in local folklore. A farmer tried to kill the Brownie but it evaded his attack and explained that, in return for being allowed to stay on the land, it was willing to work on the farm. The Brownie no longer wanted to live in the sea, tired of gnawing the bones of drowned men.

As much as it is bleak, Copinsay is also dizzyingly beautiful. To the north is the even smaller, inaccessible Horse of Copinsay – the Norse liked to zoomorphise small islands – with cliffs rising straight out of the sea. A flock of more than fifty puffins is swimming near the coast, with more perched on the clifftop among the sea pinks. The view from the the clifftop, back down the steeply sloping island to the farmhouse, across a curving tidal causeway joining three low holms to the Mainland beyond, under immense skies, is one of the best in Orkney.

Until around 1914, brave and hungry islanders took part in 'fowling' on Copinsay, catching seabirds from the cliffs for their flesh, eggs and feathers – known as 'swappin' for auks', in Orcadian dialect. These days, the birds are caught only for conservation research. I go out with Juliet and Yvan around Copinsay's cliffs and geos, looking for birds. They catch shags by extending an eight-foot fishing pole down the cliff to their nests: Yvan loops the bird in a kind of noose, lifts it and passes it up to Juliet, who grapples it, flapping and honking, and puts a bag over its head. A GPS tag is carefully taped to the feathers on its back and, over the next few days, every hundred seconds the tag will communicate with satellites and plot the shag's location. The operation is efficient and the shag is quickly released but they will have to catch the same bird again in the next week to collect the data – about how far and where it has been to feed – which will contribute to biological records and inform government marine policy.

Having a small island to myself brings a strange mixture of freedom and confinement. I have a pee on the edge of a cliff looking out towards Norway and feel like a Viking conqueror. A year ago I was in rehab in London. Now I'm lying star-shaped in the centre of the helicopter pad built to service the lighthouse, with its shadow over me, and bonxies – the Orcadian name for great skuas – above, on an uninhabited island in the North Sea. I walk back down the hill, fall asleep for an hour in a sheltered spot by the bay and dream of being a seabird on a high ledge.

I plan to walk around the whole island but my circumnavigation is thwarted by the birds. Near the cliff edge, bonxies launch a dive-bomb attack, protecting their nearby nests. I hear one repeatedly swishing just above me and cover my head with my hands, duck and move swiftly out of the area.

I cross the tidal causeway to Corn Holm and suddenly the cold farmhouse feels relatively civilised. I am the first human here in weeks and my arrival flushes gulls and greylag geese into the sky. Big, threatening black-backed gulls circle above; fulmars shift and squawk in their nests, some expelling foul vomit in my direction. Turning onto Ward Holm, I hear a noise like a sound effect for a B-movie haunted house – echoing moans and ghoulish howls – and it takes me a moment or two to realise I have come across a colony of grey seals basking on the rocks. At the sight of me, the huge mottled grey mammals slide into the water but don't swim away. They turn around and every pair of eyes is on me.

I start to worry that the tidal window for crossing the causeway will close and I'll be stranded. I cut my route short and don't venture to the ominously named Black Holm. Although I haven't met the Brownie, I feel spooked. When the people left, Copinsay became the birds' island. I am on their territory and won't stay too long.

I want to find out more about life on uninhabited islands so I go to Westray to visit Marcus Hewison. Although he has always lived on Westray, Marcus farmed the abandoned island of Faray for thirty-nine years, renting the grazing of the three-hundred-acre island and its hundred-acre holm from the Stewart Foundation, part of the Church of Scotland. At his house, I am fed with home bakes as he tells me how he kept up to six hundred ewes on Faray, getting over to them in his own yoles. He is one of the few farmers, these days, with sea as well as land skills, which used to be the norm when Orcadians were known as 'crofters with nets'. With the yole moored at a geo, access to the island, for both people and animals, was a scramble up the rocks. Marcus used to spend two or three weeks a year at lambing time on Faray, staying in the old schoolhouse with a couple of helpers.

Although there are eleven houses on Faray, no one has lived there full time since 1947. A few of the island's past residents, now very elderly, are still alive on the Orkney Mainland. When Marcus first visited the island, the schoolhouse windows were broken and birds and sheep had been getting in. The five-hundred-strong black-backed gull colony had to be controlled as 'they were taking the lambs' tongues before they were out of the ewes'.

Marcus was always trying new things on Faray and once introduced six red deer to the island. Although there are no longer any deer in Orkney, antlers have been found, so it was a reintroduction attempt. Deer are notoriously difficult to contain but Marcus thought putting them on a small island might be the answer. Not long later he got a phone call saying the deer were on neighbouring Eday – they had swum more than a mile across the sound. He describes how he went to Eday and drove the deer down to the beach, lassoed them and tried to get them into the boat. Not all the deer were caught and some later swam further to Green Holm; one was drowned.

There are no rabbits or rats on Faray, just mice, and once Marcus had a 'notion' to put a hare over there. For six months he didn't see it again until he went over in the snow and found footprints: 'I went around a corner and there he was.' The hare survived for some years and was eventually taken back to Westray.

At an Orkney auction mart sale, Marcus sold lambs off Faray for the last time. 'I've stopped Faray on a high,' he says, 'with the best price I've ever got for a pen of Suffolk cross lambs.'

Hamish Haswell Smith's *Scottish Islands*, a hefty book with detailed maps, careful illustrations, and information on access and anchorages, is often regarded as the Bible for island lovers, or islomaniacs. I flick through it, cross-referencing with Wikipedia and Google

Maps. I also keep going back to the 'Lonely Isles' website, a catalogue of uninhabited and sparsely populated Scottish islands, and dream of visiting these places, wondering what life there used to be like.

Like Hether Blether, the abandoned islands are imaginary in a way, so seldom visited that they exist more in books, stories and memories than in daily life, when they are often just a blur out to sea. They have a powerful hold on the imagination. The film *The Edge of the World* was shot on the Shetland island of Foula but set on a fictional Hebridean isle under threat of depopulation. Here, catching sight of the Mainland meant bad luck and 'The hills of Scotland!' is an ominous cry throughout the film.

The true stories of depopulation are gripping. Often the Second World War was a turning point: some men left the islands for the forces and links to the outside world were opened up. As roads grew more important than sea transport for trade, the position of Scottish islands became more peripheral. This wave of depopulation is echoed in some of the problems that smaller islands have today. When communities can no longer sustain a school or shop, they become less attractive places for others to stay in or move to. There needs to be enough working-age people to carry out essential jobs and manage transport links. Like the Groat children, I left the island where I was raised. The temptations of the lifestyles elsewhere are still hard to resist.

On the smaller Orkney islands, you are limited not just by the coastline but in ways to earn a living, leisure pursuits, the weather and choice of friends. Lives are much more comfortable than in the early twentieth century, when Copinsay and Faray were abandoned, and islanders have plenty of goods, services and communications at their disposal, but many island communities are still teetering on the brink of sustainability.

I had a great drive to leave and experience more elsewhere but, like many young Orcadians, I've returned. Now I'm back I'm seeing my home anew and wondering if I should join the effort to keep the isles alive. When I am in London, Orkney itself seems imaginary. I find it hard to believe that this life is real when I'm down there. And imagination is important here. These islands could be bleak, unpromising places if it weren't for enchantments such as the porpoise, rising like Hether Blether in the offing, always just beyond our reach.

13

LAMBING

Last week Dad went to check on a ewe he'd left to give birth an hour or so before, due to have triplets. He was surprised to find only one lamb with her, then realised the other two were under her body – she'd crushed the two larger ones to death, leaving only the runt. That day the tiny lamb began shitting blood and it became apparent that the mother had stood on him as well, damaging his insides in an unknown but terrible way that soon proved fatal. The sheep was identified as a bad mother and sprayed with a red X, meaning she will not be kept until next year.

Lambing season is the best time of year on the farm but is by turns delightful and grotesque, sweet and sour. I'm still in Orkney as spring approaches and decide I will stay a bit longer as Dad's lambing assistant. The job applications I've sent with dwindling enthusiasm to London have been unsuccessful and I realise I'm also a little scared of returning. Being on the island,

and within that the farm, has seemed to help me stay safe and sober. By not drinking one day at a time, I have now been sober for more than a year, something back then I could not have believed would happen.

I do the early-morning shift, like Mum used to when she and Dad were the lambing team, getting dressed in the dark, then going out to the byre. I sleep on the sofa in the caravan. Dad has been up into the night and leaves notes for me at four or five a.m., detailing the latest lambs and things to watch out for. In the pen I look for ewes that have had lambs in the last hours, sometimes sorting out ten newborns between five confused mothers and putting them into individual pens.

We have around 220 ewes, scanned to carry an average of 1.8 lambs each. Most will give birth unassisted but the occasional ewe will need help: to pull out a large single with its head stuck or to untangle the legs of twins or triplets – a job I would sometimes be called on to help with as a child because my hands were smaller than Dad's.

Every hour I do my rounds of the shed and the field. My eyes dart to their back ends: I'm keen not to miss any signs of lambing, looking out for sheep who are pointing in a different direction from the flock, lying on their own, or walking in circles, crying out with confusion. Ewes in birth throes arch their backs downwards, like plucked strings, noses to the rafters. If a sheep has not given birth after an hour or two, I'll wake Dad to come and help.

While the ewes are let out to graze in the afternoon, I am able to bed down their pens. I shake out new bales of straw over the old, which has got dirty and compacted, while listening to rap on my headphones, enjoying being a rural farmworker listening to urban music. I take breaks in the only place on the farm I can get mobile reception: sitting on an upturned bucket out in a field, texting and posting online with sheep shit on my wellies and straw in my socks.

I remember lambing when I was a kid as hectic and disorganised, with sheep getting loose and gory tragedy, but over the years, the system has been streamlined and good behaviour bred into the flock. They come when called, slow and heavy with lambs, following each other into the big shed for the night.

Across the field I spot a newborn lamb and, as I get closer, realise it must be dead, lying limp and still. The birth sac is still across its body and head, so with my fingers I puncture it at the mouth and peel it off, like a condom. The lamb immediately sneezes, shakes itself and breathes deeply before letting out a healthy baa. The mother, who had given up and wandered away, is alerted by the sound and trots back to begin licking her newborn. In just a few minutes it will be walking and sucking, and tomorrow skipping around the field.

At lambing time I'm part caring midwife, part stern eugenicist. Because sheep have only two teats, ewes who have triplets must usually have one 'fostered', as we call it, but really it's more of a forced adoption. I feel like a 1950s doctor as I line up three lambs to choose the largest to take away. A ewe scanned to have a single has begun to give birth: as soon as her lamb is born, it is dunked in a bucket of warm water along with its new foster-sibling; then they are stirred up together in a bloody brew with the afterbirth and fluids so that they take on the same smell before being presented to the post-natal mother. Occasionally the imposter is detected and rejected but in the majority of cases the deception is a success.

Between the lambs, there are other jobs – building up more broken dyke, cutting down rogue thistles, feeding the poultry that peck around the farmyard. At the end of the day I attend to my body, thinking of how it will function rather than how it looks: getting rid of any hangnails that could get caught, letting the hot shower massage my muscles.

A weak lamb that can't walk and is too weak to suck is taken inside, given some milk in a tube pushed gently down its throat and into its stomach. When Mum was here and we still lived in the farmhouse, we used to put them in a cardboard box in the oven and after a few hours they would either be dead or warmer and strong enough to go back to their mothers. Snuffling lambs are sweet and milky in the hay.

I walk up to the Outrun to check the sheep with older lambs that have already been moved up from the fields closer to the house. The sun moves in and out of the clouds, casting rippling shadows on the short grass. The treeless landscape is laid out in gently curving horizontal stripes of grassland, cliff, sky and sea, so it is easy to spot the dead lamb, far away from the flock. Its eyes and innards have been pecked out by gulls and it is splayed, like a rug. I turn it over with the tip of my welly to note if it's a ram or a ewe. The number we spray on the side of twins has become too blurred to read but at least this means the ewe has another lamb to take her milk.

Most lambs are healthy, and we simply spray their navels with a squirt of yellow iodine to prevent infection and carry them out onto the grass by the front legs with a finger between, the way I was taught, while they squirm reassuringly and their mothers follow.

On fine spring days the landscape glows, lambs play under the wild, bubbling song of curlews and lapwings and, further away, the sounds of the sea and the odd tractor at neighbouring farms. But when it rains the yard gets muddier and the grass barer, the sheep huddle behind the dykes and I can't hear much but the wind through my woolly hat.

These lambs born in April will either be sold in autumn as 'store' for another farmer to feed up, or over winter as 'fat', shipped to abattoirs in the south. 'Scottish Organic Lamb' sold in Tesco nationwide might have come from our farm.

About ten years ago, my parents converted the farm to organic, a system based around not using synthetic fertilisers. There are also certain rules about medication, which should be reactive only, no routine dosing, and animal welfare. We were no longer allowed to keep our cows chained up inside over the winter and they were replaced with long-haired, horned red and black Highland cattle hardy enough to stay out all year. We stopped castrating the lambs, meaning ram and ewe lambs are now separated after weaning, and abandoned traditional tail-docking, finding no problems with fly infestations on dirty tails.

It took several years of chemical-free farming before the farm and its produce could be certified organic and Dad has an inspection each year. He now uses crab waste from the local shellfish factory, mixed with straw, muck and seaweed, as a natural fertiliser. Spread on the barley, oats and reseeded grass, this mix helps to hold moisture, minerals and earthworms in the soil, rather than simply layering on synthetic nitrogen fertilisers, a by-product of the oil industry. Clover added to the mix of seed for new grass also acts as a natural fertiliser. Using these methods, grass and crop yields haven't decreased as much as expected.

I remember the smell of the fish pellets we used to give the in-lamb ewes and also the smell of the sheep dip. The dip next to the Bay of Skaill has now been filled in and made into a windswept picnic area. One by one the ewes were plunged into the chemical swimming pool, pressed down to make sure their wool became impregnated, to protect against parasite infestation. I was tied up nearby, like a dog, to make sure I didn't run and fall into the acrid and enticing brew.

It's only lately I've been able to see beyond the dirt and hard work to some of the benefits of the farming lifestyle. When I was small, both my parents worked at home. From the kitchen window I could see someone crossing the field in overalls and wellies: they could be either Mum or Dad. Dad has always kept a notebook of jobs to do: buying feed or fixing the chainsaw were on the same list as repainting the bathroom in the house.

The whole family would take part in things like haymaking. When we were small, Tom and I would play in the fields when the adults were working, warned not to get too close to the tractors and balers. When we were older we had to help, stacking the bales of hay into 'stooks' in the field, lifting and restacking them on the trailer, then throwing them off into the byre when we got back to the farm. A whole hayload, the size of a small house, with us kids, Mum, helper and the dog, once tumbled down onto the road as the tractor turned a sharp corner. The bales cushioned our fall.

At the end of the lambing season, all the sheep and lambs are moved from around the farm up to the Outrun and other top fields – a job requiring help. I vividly remember the days when we gathered the flock into a group at the corner of the field, then pushed them up the track. Ewes with new lambs become fearless and don't flock in the usual way: staring down sheepdogs and stamping their feet. There was chaos as lambs escaped, dogs and kids sent to run after them as they scattered in panic or sheer exuberance.

As on many medium-sized farms, there have been different diversifications and experiments over the years. Dad went to other farms to shear their sheep and took in shearing blades for sharpening, using a dangerously spinning disc of sandpaper, a job I was taught and did for the customers the last time Dad was in hospital when I was a teenager. We had ducks and chickens, and a succession of Border collie sheepdogs. We had a goat, two horses, semi-wild cats and a changing herd of about ten kye. These days, Dad keeps a few alarming-looking and -sounding guinea fowl, the odd Kunekune pig and fifty thousand honey bees.

⋆   ⋆   ⋆

On the farm we were always close to both birth and death. Lambs were skipping around the field and a few months later hefty carcasses were hanging in our playroom in the house, a few kept back from the abattoir for our family and friends to eat. Often there was drama and stress. Animals would escape down the track and be found elsewhere in the parish. An expensive newly bought ram would die before it had a chance to carry out its duty, either by fighting with other rams or because it was over-bred and weakly. Now, newly introduced rams are put in a tightly packed pen for a couple of nights so they can't kill each other by fighting where they have enough room to charge. But there are always new worries on the farm. Recently, there is the threat of change with the visiting surveyors representing energy companies from the south.

As well as the farm work, I recall unexpected interactions with wild animals: a swan in the freezer that died flying into a power line; a sparrowhawk found inside the tractor cab; glimpses of otters moving between the sea and a small freshwater loch.

At school, the question wasn't which football team you supported but which make of tractor was your favourite: John Deere, Case, Massey or Ford. But I never joined the Young Farmers. I read music and fashion magazines and American novels. Now, browsing the internet in my tea break, still in my padded boiler suit, I suddenly feel frustrated, like I did when I was a teenager: I want to wear a dress and go into town but I can't. I need to go and check on the lambing shed.

Carrying lambs out to the fields, I pass the farmhouse and remember the comforting weight on the corner of my bed,

Mum or Dad tucking me in. The creaks of that old house grew into me as firmly as the wind outside, and sometimes in London, waking in the night, I would think I was still there – the chinks of light through the wooden stairs above my bed, the rain on the window behind my head and my bare feet on the cold flagstones.

The Jobcentre had been patient but was now putting pressure on me to find work and widen my job hunt from office jobs in London. Reluctantly, I begin looking in the situations-vacant page of the *Orcadian* each week. I spot an advert for a summer job working on a bird conservation project for the RSPB and, although I was pretty sure I'd be back in my real life in London before long, something about it appealed to me and I thought it wouldn't hurt to send off an application.

14

THE CORNCRAKE WIFE

IT IS TWO A.M. ON Friday night and I'm alone down a farm track, dancing in the glow of my headlights because I heard the call I know belongs to a medium-sized brown bird. Unexpectedly, I got the job working for the RSPB on the Corncrake Initiative, a long-running conservation project and, rather than return to London, signed a contract for a summer in Orkney.

I spent the summer staying up all night. When everyone else was asleep, I was out in the gloaming with the livestock and the wildfowl, searching for a rare, endangered bird: the corncrake.

Corncrakes, sometimes known as landrails, are similar in size and shape to moorhens, but brown with a ginger wing and pink beak, inhabiting farmland rather than wetland. At one time they were common across the whole of the UK. Numbers declined dramatically in the twentieth century, and now they are found only on the western isles and Orkney in this country. The birds are on the Red List of threatened species of the International Union for Conservation of Nature, and last summer, 2011, just thirty-one calling males were located here.

My job is to locate every calling male – only the males call – in Orkney. I appeal for public reports, asking people to call my 'corncrake hotline' if they hear one. My answerphone message contains a recording of the call so that people can compare it with what they have heard. The sound is like a credit card being scraped over a comb, or a guiro percussion instrument or, like the corncrake's onomatopoeic Latin name, *Crex crex*. The oldest islanders are already familiar with the call, which was once the sound of the countryside on summer nights.

As well as collecting other people's reports, I carry out my own comprehensive survey. It is lucky that I've just got my driving licence back after the ban for drink-driving because my survey is carried out by car between midnight and three a.m. Corncrakes call throughout the night, peaking between these hours when the males are at the centre of their territories. Over seven weeks, following a standardised national methodology, I survey twice every one-kilometre map-grid square in Orkney containing suitable corncrake habitat – hay and silage fields, and tall vegetation such as nettles or iris. Corncrakes are elusive. They hide in the long vegetation and we locate them by ear, rather than sight. I stop every 250–500 metres, wind down the windows and listen for two minutes.

Now that lambing has finished, I've come back to stay at Mum's in Kirkwall and she's already in bed when I leave the house around eleven – nightclub time – having filled my Thermos with coffee rather than wine, dressed in warm layers, made sure I have my maps and phone charged, and drive out into the countryside. I pass homes putting their lights out for the night, then ancient standing stones and modern wind turbines on the dark hillsides.

At this time of year in Orkney – the weeks around midsummer – it barely gets dark overnight: the sky just dims. This time between sunset and sunrise is known as the 'simmer dim' or the 'grimlins', from the Old Norse word *grimla*, which means 'to twinkle or glimmer'. I feel like the only person awake on the island, and am usually the only driver on the road. On a clear night with little cloud, there is a perpetual sunrise or sunset during the hours of my survey.

I am lucky to have an excuse to stop and listen. It takes a few seconds for the car's engine to stop running and quieten, then for my personal velocity to come to a halt, heartbeat to slow, clothes to stop rustling, for the noise in my head to fall away and the sounds of the night to reveal themselves. I become dark-adjusted and alert to noise: chin on the open window, cool wind on my face, occasionally catching my reflection in the wing mirror, ears held forward by my woolly hat into prime listening position. Two minutes can seem a long time when you're concentrating.

Even at one a.m. – the darkest point of the night in British Summer Time – the birds are going bonkers. I hear the 'classic three' Orkney birds – bubbling curlews, piping oystercatchers and lapwings, which sound like a dial-up modem – nearly every time I stop. I note down unfamiliar calls to ask my knowledgeable colleagues back in the RSPB office: 'creaking bedsprings', 'haunted chicken'. They inform me that the 'shivery baby goat' sound I hear is snipe 'drumming', an eerie, memorable wobble made by its tail feathers. There are other noises too: of wind turbines, domestic animals and livestock, a flowing burn, the sea, wind and rain. I learn that, although I can't see much on foggy nights, sound travels further in the mist.

The sun both rises and sets north-ish at this time of year, just dipping below the horizon, so surveying the north coast is particularly special. Speeding home, just getting light, the currents of Eynhallow Sound are churning through the mist. I park at the top of Wideford Hill next to the communications pylons and look down at the lights of Kirkwall.

I can go for nights without hearing a corncrake. The weather gets into the car. On the rare occasions I see another vehicle I wonder what they're doing out in the country at this time of night, and they think the same about me. A few times farmers, and once a police car, ask me what I'm doing but I have a good reason. At times I'm scared, down an unfamiliar country road alone at night, shocked by a scarecrow. I'm connected to the world through my phone, Google Maps helping me navigate in the dark. On Friday and Saturday nights, I think about what my friends are doing back in London, reading their drunk tweets before they delete them in the morning. The survey can become monotonous, but when I'm flagging, the sky does something amazing. I love the mist that hangs below me in Orkney's gentle valleys, as if I've climbed to the top of the beanstalk.

In the bottom right-hand corner of my photograph is a pair

of bright flashes – the eyes of a sheep I hadn't even realised was there when I pointed my phone camera into the night. Livestock are close by, dark and quietly chewing. I've caught a goose, a hare and a teenager in my headlights. I caught the full moon in my wing mirror. I drove to the edge of the cliff, trying to get closer to the sky, looking out to smaller islands, with their light-houses glowing, flashes of colour in the dark, reflected on Scapa Flow. I share the night with cats – their eyes shining in the dykes – voles and hedgehogs.

According to the timestamp on my photograph, it was 1.08 a.m. when I saw noctilucent cloud for the first time, on a back road in the Stenness area. I knew its visibility was limited to more northern latitudes, the weeks around midsummer and late nights, so I had a chance of seeing it when out doing the corn-crake surveys. Tonight there it is, at the top of my field of vision, unmistakable. Fifty miles high, in the deep twilight, icy blue wisps hang like lightning crossed with cotton wool. I get out of the car and hold my phone to the sky, smiling like a nutter. At this time of night most clouds are silhouetted but the space cloud – it shines.

I am in perpetual hope. I want to hear corncrakes at each stop and briefly mistake for its call the quack of a duck, the churning of the blades of a wind turbine, the rasping breathing of a cow. But although I have heard quite a few, I have not seen one yet. They are extremely secretive birds, hiding low in the long grass.

In his poem 'The Landrail', John Clare describes the phenomenon of birds that can be heard but rarely seen as 'like a fancy every-where/ A sort of living doubt'. I begin to doubt my belief in corncrakes.

When I do find a corncrake – on a still night, they can be heard a kilometre away – it's almost too much to believe. I get out of the car and, keeping to the road so I don't disturb the bird, lit by the grimlins and my headlights, I move slowly towards the call until I can pinpoint its location by ear.

In my confusion I don't know where I am. Dusk blends into dawn and I can't say whether the day is ending or beginning. Then I'm confused by the sight of a cruise ship, all lit up out to sea, like a tower block floating in space.

But the light – by three a.m. I don't need the car light to read my map – reveals where I have been all along. It's just my familiar island. Surveying the West Mainland in particular, each road is full of memories. I stop at the former post office where my birth was registered while Dad was in hospital, at the school bus stop where I often found four-leaf clovers, at the passing place near Yesnaby where the police caught me drink-driving. I've driven thousands of miles within a fifty-mile-diameter island. I have driven all of Orkney's roads and traversed its tracks, grooved its geography into my mind, its contour lines onto my skin, making it more difficult to leave again.

I have had to visit some of the smaller Orkney islands and I travel to them on the roll-on, roll-off – 'ro-ro' – car ferries that run on bacon butties and in nearly all weathers. On Sanday, I see a couple walking their ferrets off the ferry, hear two male corncrakes call in competition from either side of a loch, and a story about a cow that swam a mile. I'm told on Stronsay about a corncrake that got caught in a lobster creel. On Eday, where there are no corncrakes, I hear about how fishermen on the isles didn't want to learn how to swim so that if the boat went down they would drown more quickly. On Burray, the haar comes in but the fog turns pink in the sunrise and I can hear seals, across the fields, down on the shore, howling like ghouls.

As I drive, I try to unpick what happened: all the houses I've lived in, the lost jobs, the treatment centre, my aching heart. At first, I counted the days I had been sober, then the weeks. Now it's just the months and the cravings come less frequently, but they still come. Driving home in a beautiful dawn, the only person on the road, listening to happy hardcore, I feel like the Queen of Orkney. Then, suddenly, all I want is a bottle of wine and it's a good thing the island has no twenty-four-hour off-licences.

The main reason for the decline in numbers of corncrakes over the twentieth century is increasingly mechanised farming methods, in particular larger and more efficient grass mowers. Most corncrakes live in fields intended for hay or silage and when the mowers come to cut the grass, the birds – particularly the chicks – are usually killed. Corncrakes move away from the mower into the ever-decreasing area of uncut grass, and are eventually caught in the middle of the field and mown to death on the final swathe.

Once I've located the corncrakes, through reports from the public and my night surveys, I visit the landowners. I feel nervous driving down unfamiliar tracks, knocking at farmhouse doors, dogs barking. Older Orcadians tend to refer to women, regardless of marital status, as 'wives' so, arriving at farms to speak to farmers about the endangered birds on their land, I am announced with 'The corncrake wife is here.' The RSPB offers the farmers money to delay cutting or grazing the grass, or to mow in a 'corncrake-friendly' pattern: from the inside of the fields outwards, giving the birds more of a chance to escape. Every farmer is willing to discuss the options with me. I find them knowledgeable about the wildlife on their land and most are able to change the mowing pattern, although delaying the crop until August is often, despite the payment, too drastic a change. No one flat-out refuses: that's not really the Orcadian way. They just say they'll think about it, then I never hear back.

I learn as much as I can about this one species. I read scientific papers and follow research on their migration routes. They're all that people ask me about. I accidentally replace other words with 'corncrake' when I'm typing; I change my ringtone to a corncrake's call; I set a Google alert for corncrake references in the world's media. Somehow this bird has become my thing. I am hallucinating a *Crex crex* call in the background of music on the radio and at night I dream of corncrakes.

In June 2011, fifty adult male corncrakes were caught on the Hebridean island of Coll, lured into nets by a taped call of what they thought was a rival male. Geolocators, weighing less than a gram, were attached to their legs on plastic rings. The following summer, some of the birds were re-caught, and their tags revealed that they had travelled all the way to the Democratic Republic of the Congo in Central Africa. This seems incredible: in Scotland, corncrakes are reluctant to fly at all, which is what makes them so vulnerable to farm machinery. There is even local folklore about them going 'underground' instead of migrating, turning into moorhens or perhaps riding on other birds' backs. But fly they do, although just 30 per cent of adults survive the migration to return to Orkney the following year. Many are trapped in hunters' nets in north Africa. Corncrakes need to rear a lot of chicks just to replenish the population, let alone increase it.

Since before I started the job, I've been reading *Moby-Dick*. I've been reading it for so long it feels like I've been on a three-year round-the-world whaling trip, carrying it back and forth every day, hefty in my shoulder bag, like a harpoon. I'm storm-crazed Captain Ahab, but instead of a whale I'm chasing an elusive bird. Although I've heard almost thirty males, I still haven't seen one. The corncrake is always just beyond me.

On tough nights, I start to ask myself questions. Why save this bird, a bird seldom seen, a relic from the crofting times, a bird unable to adapt to modern land use? What difference does it make? And then I learn that, in 1977, corncrake remains were excavated from the Pictish and Viking Age site at Buckquoy, in Orkney's West Mainland. It shocks me to discover that corncrakes had been here for thousands of years, yet in less than a century we have all but wiped them out. Their decline is undoubtedly down to human activity so it seems right that we should take responsibility to conserve the last few.

An isolated male, perhaps the only corncrake on his island, calls for three, four, five hours a night, for months. One was heard calling on Flotta all summer, and I am delighted to learn that chicks were seen at the end of the season – he found a mate, after all.

I reach a total of thirty-two calling male corncrakes heard in Orkney during the season, just one more than last year. Each male that calls from the same spot for more than a few days is assumed to be accompanied by a female. Although numbers still remain low, since the RSPB's Corncrake Initiative has been running, there has been a slight upward trend in Orkney. Unlike the fabled drowning sailors, the corncrakes are struggling against death and somehow it is as if my fate becomes intertwined with that of the bird. I'm trying to cling to a normal life and stay sober. They are clinging to existence.

My friend told me about when her mother died, leaving behind a husband and three young children. The family went on holiday in America, and my friend described her dad as 'just driving'. You might feel that you can't go on, yet you do, just driving to give yourself something to do while things settle, shift and gain form, until the way that life is going to be makes itself clear. I'm driving on, one-kilometre grid square by one-kilometre grid square. Imperceptibly, the churning in my chest is subsiding. Like when I cycled at night in London, I find relief by being in motion. One night, I realise I'm feeling easier and more normal, even lucky to live and work here in Orkney.

This is a different kind of nightlife. The life I had in the city – parties and clubs – is no longer there for me but these never-nights, marking off grid references and following maps in the mist, they are my own. I've found no corncrakes tonight but dawn is coming, I've got a flask of coffee and I can hear seals.

There are wonderful moments. I make eye contact with a short-eared owl, plentiful this year and known locally as 'catty faces'. It's on a fence post next to where I park, and we both turn our heads and see each other. I gasp, the owl flies. One still-pink dawn, just before midsummer, I stop at the Ring of Brodgar on the way home. There's no one around, and I take all my clothes off and run around the Neolithic stone circle.

Then, just after three a.m., when I finish my survey one night towards the end of the seven weeks, I pull away slowly in the car and something unexpected happens: I see a corncrake. It's just a moment but it's in the road right in front of me, running into the grass verge. Its image – the pink beak and ginger wing – keeps darting through my mind: just a second that confirmed the existence I'd spent months searching for. My first and only corncrake. Usually dawn comes slowly but tonight I drive out of a cloud and suddenly it's a new day.

15

ROSE COTTAGE

VISITING THE SMALLER ISLANDS FOR the corncrake surveys
I get to know their individual landscapes, from fertile agricultural Shapinsay, to the moors of Hoy – 'the high island'. There
are twenty inhabited Orkney islands, with populations ranging
from two to hundreds. On these islands there are often more
houses than people now: low 'butt and ben' crofts, some derelict,
some carefully restored and updated; caravans held down against
the wind by ropes and breeze blocks; and farms, from small and
old-fashioned to modern and slick. Studying maps and driving,
past rusting vehicles and abandoned baths at the side of the road,
I notice odd farm names, often with their roots in the Norn
language that was once spoken, and often repeated on different
islands: Woo, Queer, Balaclava, Windywalls, Patience, Flaws, Crook.

Almost against my will, I'm becoming more interested in
learning about and visiting these places and have now been to
all of the inhabited islands but three: archaeology-heavy Wyre;

Auskerry, home to just one family who changed their surname to Auskerry; and Papa Stronsay, where the only inhabitants are a community of monks, the Sons of the Most Holy Redeemer.

It's surprising to me that, after the corncrake season finishes and they have migrated back to Central Africa, I choose to go even further from the city: I'm spending the winter on Papa Westray, known as Papay, the most north-westerly and one of the smallest inhabited Orkney islands, just four miles long by one mile wide with seventy residents. Papay is a long, thin island. In map form, it looks a bit like a Wotsit, or an old man with a walking-stick, vomiting. I'd visited in the summer to help the RSPB count rare *Primula scotica* and liked the place, sensing a friendly community proud of their beautiful island.

An air service operates between Kirkwall and the north Orkney islands of Papay, Westray, Eday, Sanday and North Ronaldsay. The smallest and most northerly of these islands, Papay and North Ronaldsay, where ferries arrive just once or twice a week, are particularly reliant on the plane. The island's teenagers make the twenty-minute journey to Kirkwall on Mondays and Fridays, attending the secondary school and staying in the halls-of-residence during the week.

Early one morning in mid-November, before it is light, Mum drops me off at Kirkwall airport. At the North Isles desk, the pilots and airport staff know most of the passengers by name. There are no queues or passport checks: we just walk across the runway, the same runway from which Dad was taken to hospital the day I was born, and use a step to enter the eight-seater propeller plane. Inside, there is no division between the passengers and the pilot – he simply turns in his seat to tell us to put on our seatbelts. Being in such a small aircraft feels like being in a car in the sky. As we rise, I grip my seat. Day is breaking. We pass over the town and see fishing boats and ferries below. We fly over Thieves Holm, an uninhabited skerry to which witches and criminals were once banished, and over the now-uninhabited Hellier Holm with its lighthouse, over Shapinsay and its Victorian castle, and Egilsay and the Norse kirk where St Magnus was executed.

I relax. It's a privilege to travel like this and I feel good when I'm going somewhere. The movement of the plane settles me and I think about what I'm doing. I've been back in Orkney for most of a year but still often feel off-kilter and ill-tuned. It is time to find my own place but this time I'm going north, not south. I want to experience life on a very small island, smaller than the Orkney Mainland with its two small towns. On Papay I know I'll be part of a small community of seventy, bound together by sharing a limited area of land. I want to find out if anything else binds the people. My living costs will be low and a winter in my own house, close to the sea, will be the next step in my recovery. I want the islands to continue holding me together and keeping me up.

The North Isles are spread out below and, as the sky lightens, we pass above illuminated fish farms, aquamarine bays and dark skerries before reaching Papay. The island is small, low and green, mostly split into orderly fields by dykes and fences. The sea churns white at its rocky edges, as if the island is constantly fighting off engulfment.

We land briefly on Westray before making a two-minute hop over to Papay – the shortest scheduled flight in the world. Papay's airport at first seems little more than a field and a shed. Flights are met by farmers Bobby and his brother David, who, I learn, two or three times a day break from their work, put on waterproof uniforms and drive 4x4s to the airport to attend to the plane. Jan, who lives on the island and whom I met when I was here in the summer, is waiting to meet me. I'm carrying, among other things, a bag of fire kindling, my laptop, three kilos of porridge and thermal underwear. She drives me just a couple of minutes along the road that bisects the island to the little pink house where I'll be living for the next four months.

The RSPB has a reserve on Papay and the house is the RSPB warden's cottage, named Rose Cottage for its lurid pink paint job, making it distinct from the stone and pebble-dashed houses on the island. Locally, the cottage is called 'the birdy hoose', home during summer to the 'birdy wife' or 'birdy man' but it is usually empty over the winter. I'm no longer working for the RSPB but when I realised they had a house empty for the winter and asked about it, they kindly agree to let me stay there, paying a small rent and keeping the place dry. This winter there will be a light on in Rose Cottage.

I had been warned that the house, which I've not visited before, is draughty and cold, and when I arrive, I am apprehensive. It has been empty for a few weeks and smells slightly damp, but once I get the open fire going and hang a heavy curtain over the low door to block draughts, it's really quite cosy in the kitchen. I sit in the old armchair by the fire, looking around at the mismatched paintwork and crockery. The house has no insulation so, like the caravan, it will be impossible to live here without being aware of the weather.

The cottage, built in the sixties to house workers building a 'new' (as it's still known) pier for the ferry to moor, is at the narrowest part of the island, just five hundred metres from each side to the sea. Through the two windows in the kitchen facing south and east, I can see the water surrounding the island on three sides, port, fore and starboard, and watch the sun's short southern journey as I did last winter while building dykes. Here, I will have a constant awareness that I am on an island and have been told that, in high weather, sea spray can be blown the whole way across our small strip of land.

There are objects in the house collected by the wardens who have spent summers here: shells, bones, small pieces of crockery worn down into rounded pebbles by the sea. A vertebra of a small whale hangs on the bathroom door and a perfect spherical sea urchin sits on the mantelpiece. I find dissected owl pellets containing the bones of Orkney voles, and a storm petrel wing, still carrying the distinctive and not unpleasant musky odour of the bird.

Although I'm new to Papay, I'm not new to rural island life. Rose Cottage is at the end of a farm track and the sound of a tractor passing my bedroom window is familiar. I grew up with the cycles of the farm seasons and know the daily winter feeding routine, when the hay or silage harvested in the summer is doled out to hungry livestock, and note the day the cattle are taken into the byres for the winter. Outside, I wear wellies all winter, like Dad does most of the year.

I decide that I will spend my time in the kitchen with the fire, leaving the rest of the house to the cold. From the kitchen, I see the Holm, Papay's calf island, and the creel boat belonging to Douglas, now the island's only fisherman. I can see all of the biggest North Isles apart from Stronsay. To the east is a landmass with cliffs forming three steps: 'the heads of Eday'. Further along the horizon lies Sanday, and when the sun rises, it lights the island's curves from behind, making silhouettes of wind turbines on the hilltops. North again, on a clear day North Ronaldsay is visible, so low-lying that just the houses can be seen, disembodied and floating on the sea.

On the other side of Papay, to the west, is our nearest neighbour Westray, home to three hundred people, supporting such things as a shellfish factory, a junior-secondary school and a chippie. The peedie ferry goes from Papay to Westray and back every day, carrying one teenage schoolboy and goods from the bakery. Behind Westray, the heather-clad mound of Rousay rises, and beyond that, the hills on Orkney's Mainland. I watch clouds decaying into rain or snow on the Mainland on days when it is dry on Papay.

On Papay itself, down the road along the middle of the island, beyond the airfield, is the cluster, not quite big enough to be called a village, of the post office, church, school and shop/hostel, seeming closer than it feels when I am trying to cycle there on a windy day.

At the moment there is still some green in the fields, but as the winter progresses the landscape will become more washed out and by March the view from my kitchen will be at times almost monochrome, if it wasn't for the fluorescent orange windsock at the airport. I didn't imagine I'd move to Papay and find myself in a flight path. On these winter mornings, I'm often woken by the plane descending over Rose Cottage. Sometimes it spooks every bird on the island, it seems, and I watch from my kitchen window ten or so different flocks rising at once, the sky suddenly busy with clouds of greylag geese, turnstones, golden plovers, snipe.

Having my own place again is a risk. This would be the perfect location to do some solitary drinking. I remember those nights at the kitchen table on the farm when I was working on Flotta and later in London bedrooms. Each session would take the same pattern: at two to five drinks I would be elated, feeling free and adult; but after six to ten a desperate loneliness came and I would make frantic efforts to avoid being alone. Often, in the mornings, I'd go through my phone history, text messages and emails to find out whom I'd tried to contact, looking for an audience or affection.

I went through years of hung-over days when my only aim

would be to avoid talking to anyone or having to do much work. I had a couple of hours, every day or two, of heady drunkenness and spent the rest of the time either repairing the damage done or hanging on – white-knuckling – until I could get to the shop, be alone, and start the cycle again. I am not going to fall into that unhappy unproductive pattern again. Mum said that, during these coming months on Papay, I would need to call on strengths I hadn't used before. She first moved to Orkney at the beginning of a long winter, so she knows.

Rose Cottage is like a perfectly designed halfway house, where I can have my own place and develop healthy, responsible routines, within the sheltered community of the island.

There are no flatmates or close neighbours to hear me crying at night. I worry about being the type of clueless incomer with few practical skills, who gets things wrong and can't cope in the first harsh winter. In rough weather the little concrete-block house makes noises: rain on the windows, wind shuddering down the chimney and creeping in under the door. Southerly winds are when it's coldest in the house, when draughts sneak through imperceptible cracks in the window frames.

It's been some time since anyone's touched me. This week I've seen more seals than people, noses uppermost in the bay. There is the opportunity of isolation here in our little houses down tracks, of security in the routines of island life. I used to have headaches and miss school several days a month. In drink, I found new escapes and solaces; I had hangovers and called in 'sick' to work. I was lazy and flaky but also maybe I needed those spaces to retreat to. Since I've been sober I have treated myself like a fragile object, giving myself plenty of space and simplicity, weeks spent keeping close and low.

There are things found on Mainland Orkney that we don't have on Papay: a swimming pool, a pub, a resident minister, a doctor. There are also no hares or hedgehogs here. But the mammals we do have, we have in abundance: seals, rabbits, mice. Scientists are interested in studying small island populations. The house mouse – *Mus domesticus* – on Papay was found in a study to have a difference in mandible morphology: bigger jaws than mice elsewhere. Limited to a small breeding pool, the mice evolved to suit their habitat.

I tell people I came here simply for the cheapest rent I could find. Although that isn't completely true, I didn't choose to come here to 'downsize' or 'get back to nature'. It wasn't my plan to return home for recovery, it was more that I came back for a visit and got stuck. This is where I come from, not – like most English people in Orkney – where I chose to come to. The last year has been a gradual process of saying, 'I'll just stay for a few more weeks,' for dyking or lambing, then for a few months the corncrakes, and now I've committed to a whole winter on Papay. Orkney keeps holding onto me.

I get outside every day and have set tasks to sustain myself over the winter. I've heard that, to the far north-west, you can see Fair Isle on a clear day and I scan the horizon with binoculars. I search the beach for groatie buckies, the local name for small pink cowrie shells, prized as the most special kind of shell to find. I bake bread. I photograph patterns. I pick up driftwood for the fire – best done after a full moon or a gale, the most fruitful coast depending on which way the wind has been blowing.

While I was the corncrake wife, I was busy and professional and rarely mentioned what had happened to me in the previous few years. Here, I have time and space so am able to let myself think about how and why I made the decisions I did, and in particular what made me realise that opting for rehab and total sobriety was not an overreaction to my situation.

Less than a month after I was arrested for drink-driving in Orkney, I was back in London. Although I know the attack was not my fault, it would not have happened if I had not been so drunk.

Starting in the afternoon, I met Gloria, as I often did, at the pub on the market. The stalls were packing up, revealing a debris of discarded vegetables and cardboard coffee cups. It was still afternoon but people were drunk, sitting on the kerb with pint glasses or cans from the corner shops. Gloria had recently moved to Hackney from Notting Hill after refusing to take any more money from her father. That summer she still had savings and I was pretending I was okay, acting like I still had a job.

I liked to roll the chilled glass against my face while listening to Gloria's lightly sarcastic comments about mutual friends. We talked brightly, picking out the positives in our unlikely job prospects and joking about the men we'd hurt. In the female bluster of mutual reassurance I forgot to say what I felt: that I was scared and that something was about to give.

From the market, my drinking moved on to a Vietnamese restaurant, then back to my brother's house, where I was sleeping on the sofa, to get dressed up, then the club. Someone gave me some MDMA. I tried to go home but on the bus some people – I'd never met them before – told me about a warehouse party and I joined them. It was wild, staircases full of bodies, some of whom I knew. I'd never been to the place before and it was so good. I suddenly realised that it was close to my ex-boyfriend's house and I wanted to tell him about it. I'd gone over the peak: my excited drunkenness had tipped over into recklessness and self-pity.

I stumbled to his house – he'd tried to hide his new address from me but I'd found it out – and was ringing the bell, bashing on the door, calling his phone. No answer. I was distraught. I had to get his attention. I walked on, down a side street in the vague direction of where I was staying. He asked later why I had started dressing so slutty. A car stopped beside me and, although I can't remember exactly what he said, the driver asked me to get in and I did.

It seemed as if we were driving for a long time but I was eventually picked up by the ambulance not very far from where I'd got into the car. I remember having some kind of mundane conversation about the best route and I think I asked to be taken home. I was on my phone, calling my ex, and left a message on his answerphone telling him I was in a stranger's car.

Then the driver of the car punched me in the face as hard as he could. Everything changed. I was more sober and knew I had to escape. I opened the car door but we were still moving. I later told the police that this was when I lost my shoe. He stopped, picked up a large heavy boot from the footwell and hit me over the back of the head. I knew with no doubt that he wanted to knock me out, if not kill me. There was a struggle and we were both on the ground outside the passenger door, beside the park. He began dragging me, by my ankles, into the park, towards some trees.

The only thing I remember him saying to me is 'Be quiet.' I was not quiet. I was terrified, drunk, on drugs, and had been hit hard on the head twice, but somehow I quickly sized up the situation. He was not a big man and didn't have a weapon. Although I'd never experienced violence like that before, childhood play fights with my brother came back to me and I knew I had a chance of overpowering him. I screamed for help and shouted, 'I am stronger than you, I am stronger than you,' kicking and struggling as he tore at my tights.

I saw three men coming towards me. Moments later, it seemed, we were surrounded by flashing lights and people and my attacker had gone. I had held tightly onto my mobile phone the whole time.

At the police station they took my statement and my clothes, and in the hospital they X-rayed my head. I weighed myself and was lighter than I had been since I was a teenager. My ex was there. He'd finally returned my call and run to the park. I had his attention. We went for a cigarette outside the hospital. There was a late-night pub across the road and I suggested we go over for a drink. He looked at me with disbelief and horror and told me he couldn't stay with me.

The attacker had run from the scene, leaving his car. I don't remember giving my statement to the police but apparently my description of an 'early thirties, thin white male' resulted in a swift search of the area and one wrong man being locked up for the night. My attacker was found at his own address the next day.

In the following days a police photographer came and took photos of my black eye and the bruises in the shape of fingers around my upper arms and ankles. Although the bump on my cheekbone from the punch eventually went away, I still have a scar on the back of my head from the boot. My hair grows unusually around it and sometimes I reach and touch it.

In court a few months later, I asked for a screen so I would not have to see him again. He was identified as the person responsible for a very similar attack on another young woman a few months before. While I had remained conscious after he hit me, apparently the other girl had not been so 'lucky' and was found later walking, confused, by a motorway. He was sentenced to six years' imprisonment for two counts of attempted rape.

The sea is churned up around the Holm today. I ride my bike to the shop in a cross-wind, blowing hail into me horizontally and tilting my bike. The chain snaps and I push the bike home, where an email from London upsets me, but then a different colour washes over my computer screen and I look back through the window and the sky is changing: there's a patch of blue sky above Eday and the clouds are fringed with palest pink. A flame breaks through in the fire, my heart slows to a contented rate and everything momentarily is quivering and calm.

I've been on Papay for four weeks now and it's like one of those months when I didn't leave central London. London is an island within the rest of the UK, defined and separate. In these weeks on the island, living alone, where the markers of my routine are so different and I'm enjoying the simple challenges of keeping myself warm and fed, I am learning how to behave decently in everyday life after years of confusion. My possessions are scattered. My ties and traditions are my own to make. I can choose where I will belong.

I've worn no make-up and removed no body hair. On rare days I have a visitor – Mum comes from the Mainland, Jan gives me a lift to the shop: I wonder if I should brush my hair and take the animal bones off the table. I have the odd pang for takeaways and cafés, and sometimes I can physically feel the nightlife, happening out there without me while I sit by the fire with a blanket over my knees, wondering how I suddenly became an old lady. I miss seeing and being seen and feeling close to the centre of the action. The news here is different – the weather rather than politics.

★   ★   ★

My centre of gravity has moved north. I've been thinking more about Shetland, Iceland and Faroe. I am still sometimes shocked by everything that happened, that I was in such dangerous situations, that I ended up in rehab, that I haven't drunk alcohol for twenty months, two weeks and four days and that this is how it feels. I'm back here, on these windy rocks, looking for hope in my imagination and my surroundings.

Every day on Papay, there's a moment, looking back, facing into the northerly wind, at the coastline I've just walked, for instance, when my heart soars. I see starlings flocking, hundreds of individual birds forming and re-forming shapes in liquid geometry, outwitting predators and following each other to find a place to roost for the night. The wind blows me from behind so strongly that I'm running and laughing. Calm yet alert, after a few weeks on Papay I notice that I am always pretty much aware of the height of the tide, the direction of the wind, the time of sunrise and sunset, and the phase of the moon.

I start noticing that low tides – when the rocks reaching over to the Holm are most exposed – come later twice a day, as the moon appears earlier, and I think about how they are connected. The tide is influenced not just by the earth's rotation and the positions of the moon and the sun, but also the moon's altitude above the equator and the topography of the seabed – or bathymetry – and the complicated way water moves between islands. I think about the earth's rotation, and realise that it's not the tide that is going out or the moon rising: rather, I am moving away from them.

Nearby, on the uninhabited skerry of Rusk Holm, a stone

tower with a spiralling walkway was built so that, at the highest tides, the hardy 'holmie' sheep that live there eating seaweed could climb to escape being swept away by the highest waves and drowning. Right now this little house and island is my Rusk Holm tower, somewhere I can breathe as the churning waters rise below.

16

PAPAY

ALTHOUGH PAPAY IS FAIRLY REMOTE, life here doesn't have to be isolated. Over winter there is a programme of community events. On 1 December, a Saturday, the semi-seriously named 'Papay Walking Committee' – the island is organised by many committees – has planned a walk around the whole island. We're asked to gather at the old pier at midday and to bring torches: walking the eleven or so miles will take us beyond sunset at three twenty. It's hailing and I worry that, as the over-enthusiastic newcomer, I might be the only walker, but others turn up. We set off south along the east coast, following the shoreline around jagged geos and curving bays, chasing the winter sun around the tip of the island.

Talking to people while walking is a good tactic for the anxious ex-drinker. It solves the problem of what I'm meant to be doing with my body now I'm not lifting a drink. Each person who wasn't born or bred here has their own story about how they came to Papay, refined by retelling. Some people 'fall in love' with a particular island and wait for years for a time when they can leave their lives in the south and move up. Others are attracted simply by the cheaper property prices, buying a broken-down croft house and moving here without even visiting first. Daniel tells me about his two years working on Douglas's creel boat, a job he started on the first day he moved to the island from England, with no experience. Marie tells me how she realised that, as a nurse, she could work anywhere. The Northern Isles were a good place to live so she and her husband bought a house and moved from the south of England.

Many folk on the island have more than one job: David, the farmer who meets the plane, is also a coastguard, and Anne, who lives near Rose Cottage, is the postie, a mother of four, janitor at the school and creator of beautiful delicate jewellery made from things she finds on the beach – groatie buckies and sea-polished glass.

The 1851 census recorded 371 people living on Papay. As we pass now-derelict crofts scattered along the coast, I imagine each of them filled by an extended family with many children. Our current population of seventy seems to be the critical mass for keeping amenities, like a shop and the school. Islands that don't have these things are less attractive to newcomers. Thanks to the arrival of new islanders, the population of Papay has risen from a low of fifty-something in the mid-nineties and the school now has six children.

Our islands are home to a peculiar mix of the type of eccentric, adventurous 'south folk', who would choose to move up from, say, Reading to Stronsay, and the more conservative Orcadians who can trace their family on the island back generations and have watched members move away, as well as incomers who come and go. It is a mistake to think that islanders can 'get away from it all': in such a small place we are required to have more interaction with neighbours than in a city. For the most part we get along well.

As we walk, we can hear waves breaking on the Holm, tractors, squawking gulls, piping oystercatchers and intermittent hammering at a house being renovated. We smell occasional wafts of rotting seaweed and slurry from farms. The kye are kept inside from November until May and when we walk past their byres we hear the beasts rattling and roaring. A flock of curlew intersects with a skein of geese.

On the east side, a crushed car is balanced on the edge of the cliff. A few months earlier, the owner failed in a plan for quick disposal and the evidence is there for all to see, precarious and rusting, losing parts and being corroded. A few weeks later, after a westerly gale, it has gone over, leaving just one small piece of bodywork.

The land prompts tales: of shipwrecks and caves, weather and wartime, stories told through families, taught in school or happened upon on the shore. On the flagstones near the empty farm of Vestness sit two split halves of a wrecked ship: a fishing vessel run aground when a captain fell asleep. An islander's son,

Danny, worked on that ship and jumped from the sinking vessel into an RNLI inflatable, leaving behind a box of possessions including his childhood best friend, a grey teddy bear called Sammy. Sammy has never been found.

I'm told that the lime green walls in some island houses are from tins of paint once washed up on the shore. I'm told that Papay folk are known as 'doondies', a dialect term for cod, while people from Westray are 'auks' (guillemots), from Sanday 'gruelly belkies' (porridge bellies) and from Stronsay 'limpets'. I'm shown a ten-metre section of concrete path by cliffs, once part of a wartime quarry but now a road to nowhere, and the remains of the *Bellavista*, a cargo vessel grounded in 1948, rusting on the pebbles.

Papay has at least sixty archaeological sites and the map is strewn with mysterious 'burned mounds'. The most famous site is the Knap of Howar, which, in another of Papay's record claims, is western Europe's oldest surviving settlement. These two stone dwellings, kept preserved for centuries under sand, were occupied by a Neolithic family around five thousand years ago, and are older than the Egyptian Pyramids and even Skara Brae.

I've arrived on Papay just in time for the annual Muckle Supper in early November. 'Muckle' means big and, historically, the supper is a celebration of the gathering of the last crops, in other places known as the Harvest Home. More than half of the population gathers in the hall, pots of soup are wheeled out, then plates piled with 'holmie lamb', meat from the sheep that live on the Holm. Later, there is music and traditional Scottish dancing. Some of the dances I know from school but others are unique to Papay, with strange names like 'The Eight Men of Moidart'. Mainly I sit and watch but join in for Strip the Willow.

On New Year's Eve, there is 'first footing', a tradition once common all over Scotland but now mostly forgotten due to drink-driving concerns or lack of neighbourly ties. After the watch-night service at the kirk, finishing at midnight when a handbell is rung, we proceed in a loose group around houses that are open for the night, and have food and drink on offer. The first footing carries on until morning, finishing, as the sun rises on a new year, with a fry-up at the last house at the north of the island and a game called 'bum jumping' where participants race on their buttocks. Papay is carrying on old traditions but also making new ones.

On Wednesdays, I don't have breakfast and instead fill up on delicious cheese scones and home bakes at the coffee morning in the room between the church and the doctor's surgery. Here I find out that the stone piles in some fields are 'steeves' for stooks, now listed monuments to bygone agricultural ways. We discuss where to get vegetarian haggis for the Burns Supper, plans to recreate the killing of the last great auk, now an extinct bird, by chasing an island lad around the hill with paint guns, and the mandible morphology of Papay mice.

Here I have been mixing with people of all ages and back-grounds – we have to – whereas in London I was in a bubble. I went to the city to meet new people, to expand my ideas and social circles, but ended up meeting people more and more like myself. We curated our experiences into ever narrower subsections until we were unlikely to encounter anything that made us uncomfortable.

I still have a nervousness around other people. I've been bruised by the rejection of friends and flatmates. When you've spent so long messing up, covering up and apologising, it's hard to shake the feeling that you've done something wrong and default to the secretive and even sneaky behaviour that addiction involves. I often have a flickering sense that I must have said or done something terribly misjudged.

On the east shore, the coastal path is also the road and our walking group waves at every car that passes, as is the island custom. Cars do not need to undergo the MOT test here. The island feels simultaneously lawless and crime-free. There are no police – the old 'parish handcuffs' can be seen at Holland Farm – but your movements can be watched across the treeless landscape and neighbours notice what time your curtains are open in the morning. Some people on the island claim to know everyone's car not only by sight but also by sound.

I leave Rose Cottage unlocked during this walk and every day. Someone burgling my computer or porridge would not get far and Anne the postie might drop off a book I've ordered from the internet. I remember one morning at six a.m., in London, being woken by a strange man in my bedroom. We looked at each other in silence for a moment before he grabbed my laptop from the floor beside my bed and ran out. Neither the man nor the computer was ever found.

I had heard about ninety-year-old Maggie, famous locally for driving around an ancient blue tractor well into her eighties but I'd never met her because for the last few years she had lived in sheltered accommodation over on Westray. One morning this winter her body was brought home on the peedie ferry to the island she'd left only a handful of times.

Maggie had lived alone at Midhouse since her parents died in the sixties. In her lifetime she had seen water on tap and electricity come to the island, along with domestic and agricultural technology – the washing-machine, the tractor – that removed much of the back-breaking hard work that made up island lives. She was a link back to the more self-sufficient crofting lifestyle of farming and fishing: of bringing the seaweed, or 'tangles and ware', up off the beach to dry out – some parts to be used to fertilise the land and others to be shipped south as 'kelp' for use in soap- or glass-making; of using horses and cattle to pull the ploughs; of salting and drying fish for a staple food – cuthies and sillocks – eaten with tatties.

I go for a walk on the morning of Maggie's funeral and the island is strangely still and silent – everyone else is in the kirk before going to the graveyard. It is mild for January and the wind has calmed. That evening, about five o'clock, the pressure suddenly drops, the wind rises and, overnight, Orkney is battered by the strongest gales of the winter.

The Papay Walking Committee continues its circumnavigation, back up the west edge where the sun is dropping behind Westray, and where we slide over rocks and seaweed. I turn my back to the wind to blow my nose or get my camera from my pocket. We walk the eleven miles in hail, light snow and sun, under a rainbow and over stiles. At this time of year there is a lot of marshy ground and I regret not wearing wellies.

Although snow is rare on Papay, melting quickly in the salty atmosphere, our daily lives are highly influenced by the weather. In bad weather the boat and plane may not come. I turn up at the airfield for a shopping trip to Kirkwall but the plane has been cancelled due to fog. We need to be flexible in the winter, able to adjust to downtime or do without things. It's when something goes wrong – a car or computer breaking down – that life can get more difficult. It can take a while to get new parts, and vehicles have to be winched onto the ferry and taken to mechanics in the town, an expensive business. There are different frustrations: like everywhere else in modern Britain, we have disagreements, spam email, letters from credit-card companies, unemployment, but we don't have roadside advertising, traffic jams, pollution.

Over Christmas, bad weather meant there was no ferry for a couple of weeks and the shop ran low on fresh food. The usually well-stocked Co-op is open for two or four hours a day, and going for milk often feels like a social occasion. I don't have a car so have to ask for help with things like getting sacks of coal home. I was fearful, from warnings and childhood experiences, of doing the wrong thing, being too loud, too English, but I meet only friendliness and helpfulness on Papay, as well as a gentle curiosity about what I'm doing there.

One night there is a knock at the door: an unexpected delivery of a third of a cabbage after I'd mentioned in passing in the shop that a whole cabbage was a lot to buy if you're living alone, and to carry on a bike. This small friendly gesture calmed me, helped soothe some anxiety that I wasn't fitting in. The workings of society on an island are easier to understand than in a city and I'm gradually relaxing and seeing more clearly.

I had got to the point in the city where I felt as if there wasn't room for me – there was barely room for anyone. I had fruitless job interviews, difficulty finding a room, was crushed in public transport and paid high rent. In comparison, this island is calling for people to come and live here, to the extent of having a 'trial house' where people, particularly families, can test island life before making the commitment to relocate.

Islands have to adjust their ideas of community in line with a more transient society. There will be people, like me, who come to stay for just a few months and will always have a link to the place in the future, returning for visits. An adventurous family coming to stay for just a couple of years before they move on should not be seen as a failure but, rather, a healthy part of the flow of people bringing new ways and keeping the place working. People here are often called by their house name rather than surname. The houses are familiar, in collective memory, and will outlive the people staying in them.

The sun has just set when we reach the furthest north point of Papay and in the fading twilight we can just see the white tips of the churning waves telling of the currents meeting deep below. The light of a ship out to the north of the island travels east and later the marine-traffic website tells me it's a Croatian oil tanker making its way to Estonia. Shopkeeper Amanda tells me she is obsessed with torches and has sixty or seventy. To the east, the North Ronaldsay lighthouse blinks, and a flicker further north could be either Fair Isle's lighthouse or a faint star on the horizon.

Tonight the stars are stunningly clear and numerous. We turn off our torches and walk the beach in darkness, following the Milky Way. We talk about moonbows, rainbows created at night by the light of a full moon, which my neighbour saw a few days earlier during an evening shower. On the summer nights when I was out doing the corncrake surveys there was never the deep darkness required to see the stars like this: we have to wait until winter for the dark to reveal its glories. Two bright satellites speed across. The moon glows from behind a low cloud.

We walk the east side back to our starting point at the old pier in the dark. The route has taken five hours. Completing the circuit and closing the loop feels like a ritual. We've walked the four compass points in the weather of four seasons, in light and dark. We've followed the geographical limits of our island home, marking out the little area of land we claim against the sea.

17

MERRY DANCERS

I'D SET MY ALARM FOR before dawn – six thirty a.m. – when I'd read it might be possible to see four planets in the sky at once. I get out of bed, don't turn any lights on, trying to keep my eyes dark-adjusted, and go outside with binoculars, my jacket over my pyjamas.

The Sky Map on my phone helps me look in the right direction and, to the south-west, Jupiter is shining while, to the south-east, I can see Venus. I am fairly familiar with these two, but just above Venus, appearing about one moon's distance apart, there is a more distant planet: Saturn. On Saturn, there is ringlight similar to our moonlight. On Venus, a day is longer than a year. I hope to see Mercury rising from below the horizon but low dark cloud obscures this area of sky.

I go back to bed and, through my window, clouds move across Venus and Saturn. I hear the rain start and a bull bogling before

I fall asleep again. When I wake later it's as if it had been a dream: my early-morning sleepwalk among the planets.

Last midwinter, soon after I returned to Orkney, I began for the first time to be interested in astronomy. The long winter nights up here, combined with the lack of light pollution and the open landscape without trees, tall buildings or mountains, make it an ideal location for stargazing. Under certain conditions, the Andromeda galaxy can be seen by the naked eye from here, something only possible in places with really dark skies. 'Doing some astronomy' is a good excuse for a smoker to pop outside, although it soon develops into something more than that for me.

One evening, instead of going to an AA meeting, I went to the first ever gathering of the Orkney Astronomical Society. I stopped drinking to do things, rather than to spend my time talking about stopping drinking. Since then, I've been outside at nights taking my astronomy stance: head back, mouth open, getting dizzy. On a freezing hillside in Orphir, I watched the International Space Station speed overhead. At the centre of Orkney, I sheltered behind one of the standing stones at Brodgar, and the night sky formed a glittering canopy over the low hills and dark lochs that circled me.

One morning in Rose Cottage I woke furious. I'd had a dream about being in a nightclub but feeling awkward and hating it because I wasn't drinking. I spent a decade in clubs, gigs and late-night bars and – at least for the first few years – was carried along madly by the bodies and bass and vodka. Since I'd been sober, I'd very rarely been out late, after midnight.

Sometimes I felt like I was over. I couldn't imagine how to dance sober.

In mid-December each year, while we're going about our daily routines and Christmas preparations, the earth passes through a cloud of debris left by an asteroid called 3200 Phaethon. When tiny pieces of dust and ice from this cloud hit the earth's atmosphere, at around 134,000 m.p.h., they burn up to create what we know as 'shooting stars', but of course they aren't stars at all. Meteors are what we see as shooting stars, 'ablating' as they collide with the atmosphere, creating this annual Geminid meteor shower.

For a few nights last winter I walked out alone to the outskirts of Kirkwall, beyond the streetlights, looking for shooting stars at the time of the Geminids. It was too cloudy to see any but I liked being out late in the cold, acting suspiciously, stunningly sober. This year, on Papay, around eleven thirty p.m., I take a chair and a duvet into the garden, lean back and fill my gaze with sky. There is no moon to pollute the view of the stars and it is a beautifully clear night, the Milky Way stretching out over Rose Cottage.

I've turned out all the lights in the house, even closing my laptop, so nothing spills outside. I scan the Milky Way with binoculars and count seven Pleiades. On a night like this, Orkney poet Robert Rendall described the night sky as 'tullimentan' or 'glittering'. In half an hour I see nineteen meteors, leaving streaks of brilliant light for just a second. The meteors are different sizes and brightnesses, including one so bright and low in the sky I say, 'Whoa,' out loud, but all are tantalisingly brief.

A few houses have lights on across the island, and I listen to its noises: cows moo and the occasional dog barks but mainly I hear the sea. It sounds different on either side of the island: on the east, where the North Sea meets the beach, it's a crackling crashing; but on the west, where the Atlantic collides with rocks and cliffs, it's a thundery rumble. The oceans and shore create a constant, shifting harmony, the background music to life on Papay.

Quickly, clouds move to obscure the area of visible stars and the sky is once again completely dark. When I get inside it's raining heavily.

With my wellies heavy on the ground, I'm building a picture of where I am: on earth, travelling, and what the moon, sun and stars are doing out there. In winter, the old folk on Papay would visit neighbours on the nights around full moon when there was enough light to walk home. I'm thinking about why seasons and years occur and how my personal anatomy affects my experience of it: developing spatial awareness on an astronomical scale, pushing my brain outwards. I'm learning new and pleasing information, such as that there are three stages of twilight: civil, nautical and astronomical. Nautical twilight ends when the sea is no longer distinguishable from the sky and ship navigation using the horizon becomes impossible.

I hear about how peripheral vision is best for looking into the far distance – sometimes when you look at an object directly it can disappear; and about why the stars appear to twinkle – because of atmospheric turbulence around the earth disturbing the travelling light. The light struggling to reach us is what makes it especially beautiful.

There are four freckles in a parallelogram on my left wrist and now I can see that they resemble the constellation Gemini. I think about how the moon is getting further away from the Earth and although this is only happening at about 3.78 centimetres per year, or the same speed at which our fingernails grow, it seems terribly sad.

When first I left Orkney, my friend Sean gave me a compass. I used to wear it round my neck at parties, and when people asked about it, I would tell them it was so I could find my way home. Wherever I was, north was always home. I left the compass somewhere one night. Then I was totally lost.

In Kirkwall, I discovered the best place in town for a clear view of the sky to the north: the top of the fire-escape stairway at the side of the old theatre. On nights I heard geomagnetic activity was high, I climbed up there, looking for the Northern Lights, known locally as the Merry Dancers. Usually I was disappointed but sometimes I watched the eerie glow behind the clouds.

But this winter increased solar activity is forecast, and a 'solar maximum' some time in 2013, the period of greatest activity in the sun's eleven-year cycle. When electrically charged particles expelled by the sun collide with the earth's atmosphere, lights are created, following the lines of the earth's magnetic forces, shifting and combining to create the 'dancing' effect. We are far enough north here to experience them fairly regularly, usually by looking north rather than being directly under them as you would be in the Arctic Circle.

It takes two to three days for the emissions from the sun to collide with the earth's atmosphere. On NASA's website I can see minutes'-old pictures of the sun's surface taken by the Solar Dynamics Observatory with white prominences – sunspots that could break off out into the solar system. There is aurora on other planets, I learn.

Just outside the front door of Rose Cottage, with the house lights turned out, is a perfect spot to watch the aurora: an unobscured northern vista. About 75 per cent of my view is sky, and when I tip my head back, 100 per cent. In my first couple of weeks on Papay, I see the Merry Dancers more clearly than I ever have before. I let my eyes adjust to the dark for the time it takes to smoke one cigarette then say, 'Bloody hell,' out loud. In the past I have seen a greenish-tinged, gently glowing arc, low across the north, but tonight the whole sky is alive with shapes: white 'searchlights' beaming from behind the horizon, dancing waves directly above and slowly, thrillingly, blood red blooms. It's brighter than a full moon and the birds, curlews and geese, are noisier than they usually are at this time of night, awakened by a false dawn. There is static in the air and it's an unusual kind of light, the eerie glow of a floodlit stadium or a picnic eaten in car head-lights.

Despite growing up here, I'd never taken the time to look for the Merry Dancers when I was younger. I remember my parents trying to get me to come outside on a winter night and wanting to stay in and watch *Super Ted*. I remember looking out north from the farmhouse to the sky over the Outrun, unsure if the white glow was what I was meant to be seeing. Tonight on Papay there can be no doubt.

I keep going out during the evening to see if the lights are still there, while following photos being posted online and talking with friends on the Orkney Mainland or in the south about what we are watching. I can see the aurora and so can Dad on the farm. I check the space-weather forecast – the aurora predictor. This is a geomagnetic storm of the highest order experienced in years. People on Papay ring each other up, telling their neighbours to go and look outside. The next day everyone at the coffee morning is talking about it in the excited way they would discuss unexpected good weather or a wedding.

I stay up reading about solar cycles and coronal mass ejections, about photons and poles. I read about the spacecraft and satellites monitoring the sun's potentially dangerous activity, protecting us; and alarmist predictions that energy from a solar ejection could hit our electricity networks. The Northern Lights could be a warning.

Often at night I have sat up in bed circling my ex's abandoned online profiles. On Google Streetview the branches are bare on the tree in front of the flat we used to share. I long for him to know I'm doing better but I won't be truly better until I no longer want him to know.

But tonight I'm wild on Northern Lights. I'm following a different obsession. When I visited Tom in Manchester, I walked past busy bars but didn't glance inside because I was looking up for meteors. Now, on Papay, I've gone to the Muckle Supper, first footing and even done a little dancing. I'm feeling strong enough to stay out late.

There are more solar storms forecast over the coming weeks and I will go out – maybe even after midnight – just before bed and look up, turning off my screen light, throwing away my torch and walking north into the glow. Maybe things are not going to be so bad. I've swapped disco lights for celestial lights but I'm still surrounded by dancers. I am orbited by sixty-seven moons.

18

NORTH HILL

M OST OF PAPAY IS CULTIVATED farmland and, like Orkney in general, is more fertile than its treeless and windswept first impression might suggest. The long hours of sunlight in the summer and good soil help to produce top-price cattle and high grass yields for winter fodder. But the north third of the island, the North Hill, an RSPB reserve, is different, wilder, not divided into fields and only lightly grazed at agreed times through the islanders' communal grazing rights.

I walk here several times a week. It's a similar sweep of wind-scoured, cliff-edged land to the Outrun – both are a type of habitat defined as 'maritime heathland' – and I feel at home. I am a teenager again, perched on a good lookout, writing in a notebook in fingerless gloves. These flat open coastal places are my natural habitat.

Once I get over the hill, which is a modest fifty metres above sea level and the highest point on the island, I can't be seen from any houses. I never see another person on the North Hill and I'm surrounded by ocean to the west, north and east. This winter, the heath is mine.

On the hillside there's a telegraph pole converted into a coastguards' lookout. I use the hand and footholds to climb and, as I rise, the view opens. Out to sea, white breaking waves mark the churning of the Bore, where the currents of the Atlantic meet those of the North Sea. I'm looking north, with nothing beyond the cliffs but ocean until the Arctic, and I feel like I've come to the edge of the world.

Clinging around the pole with my arms and legs, I'm in the crow's nest on a whaling boat, dreaming of seeing rare things: a snowy owl or an orca. I've been told that on a clear day I will be able to see Fair Isle on the northern horizon, perhaps even Sumburgh Head or Foula in Shetland. Spotting these distant places is apparently more likely in winter than summer when, although it may not feel like it, a heat haze can obscure vision. As I scan the horizon my eyes, used to looking at a close, glowing screen, struggle to focus. The part of the sea before the horizon is called the offing; hence ships due to arrive soon are 'in the offing'.

How far it is to the horizon depends on how high you are above sea level. If you put your eye right down to where the sea meets the beach you can't see very far. I am six feet tall, so when I look out from sea level, the horizon is three miles away but from a fifty-metre hill, raised three metres up a pole, this could increase to twenty-six kilometres.

This calculation is made more complex when the object you

are looking at beyond the horizon is itself elevated above sea level. Ward Hill on Fair Isle is 217 metres, and an observer on North Hill should be able to see it as long as it is no more than 77.8 kilometres away. I consult Google Maps, which tells me the distance between the two points is 73.2 kilometres, so it is definitely possible, if not likely, that it could be seen on a clear day. But people on the island claim to have seen 'the distinctive curved shape' of Sheep Rock on Fair Isle, which, at 121 metres high and 74.6 kilometres away, is technically too low and distant to be seen. Are the people of Papa Westray having a collective hallucination? Are they just seeing what they want or expect? Perhaps the answers can be found when the calculations are made more complex again by atmospheric refraction.

At Hogmanay Jim, who has lived on Papa Westray all his life, tells me something strange. He says that, once, for about fifteen minutes, from his house, Cott, on the east shore, he saw North Ronaldsay – not unusual, we can see it most days – but on that occasion the island was upside down, the houses and lighthouse pointing downwards towards the sea.

What Jim saw could be explained by highly unusual and specific atmospheric conditions. There is a type of 'superior mirage', called Fata Morgana, in which light is bent as it passes through layers of air at different temperatures. If there is the unusual situation of thermal inversion – a layer of cooler air below a warmer layer – an atmospheric duct can form, acting like a refracting lens, inverting what we see, which accounts for Jim's upside-down lighthouse.

Fata Morgana can result in different, changing, layers of images, inverted and right side up appearing at once. It can cause ships to be seen floating in the air. Indeed, the name comes from the legend that Arthurian sorceress Morgan le Fay cast spells to create flying castles and false lands to lure sailors to their deaths.

Jim continues with a more amazing story. On another occasion he once saw Norway and he describes the Norwegian coastline of beautiful fjords. The closest point on the Norwegian coast is around 450 kilometres from Papa Westray. Atmospheric refraction can potentially allow you to see beyond the horizon because the mirage is an elevated reflection of the real object, but seeing Sheep Rock on Fair Isle seems more likely than Norway.

A Fata Morgana can be seen yet never approached. Like Hether Blether, it always remains on the strip of the horizon.

Walking on the North Hill, I touch and turn a replica of the Westray Wife – a four-centimetre-high Neolithic figurine unearthed recently on Westray – in my pocket. AA recommends meditation, which I find hard – I get distracted, upset or fall asleep – so instead I practise my own form of contemplation by walking on the hill and absorbing my surroundings. When I walk, I am soothed by being in motion. My body is occupied and my mind free. Like the Outrun, there is more here than at first it may seem. I find a starfish at the top of the cliff; it must have been dropped by a bird. There are archaeological remains on the hill: forty burial mounds. The piles of driftwood above the high-water mark are already claimed by other islanders but I am free to collect any from below the tide line. After a westerly gale, I walk home with arms full.

The hill is studded with craters from when it was used by the Royal Navy for target practice in the Second World War and test shells were fired from ships onto the island. The holes are filled with rainwater in the winter and range from the size of a paddling pool to that of a Jacuzzi. It is said that one bomb came further south than intended and just missed a farmer's wife but killed her cow. After the war, a sailor from one of the launch ships could not believe their target island had been inhabited.

The cliffs at the east of the reserve, known as Fowl Craig, are home to colonies of seabirds at breeding time: guillemots, razorbills, puffins, shags, fulmars and kittiwakes. As in the park in Hackney, where drinkers and families became segregated into distinct noisy areas, each species has their own level on the cliffs, the puffins near the top among the rabbit holes and pink tussocks of thrift, fulmars in the top ledges and cracks, shags in big nests constructed from kelp, guillemots – social birds – further below, shuffled in together to protect their eggs from predators, with razorbills dotted between them.

In the winter the seabirds have nearly all gone, the puffins and other species out at sea where they spend the whole winter. I'm allowed to walk anywhere on the hill in winter but in summer visitors are asked to stick to the coast, leaving the hill for the colonies of Arctic terns, known locally as 'pickie ternos', that breed there. At breeding time, the terns will vigorously defend their nests, dive-bombing passers-by.

In the cottage, on the mantelpiece, there is an Arctic tern wing – it seems so small and fragile that it's hard to believe the journey it has made. Arctic terns have the longest migration of any bird, travelling back from Antarctica to Papa Westray each spring, an incredible journey of up to ten thousand miles. Local people say that the terns arrive back during 'the first fog of May'. The Arctic tern sees two summers per year and more daylight than any other creature on the planet.

The North Hill Arctic tern colony used to be one of the biggest in the UK, with up to nine thousand birds but the numbers have dropped dramatically. This summer just 213 pairs were counted on the reserve. They formed four colonies on the hill and laid eggs, but after a string of cold, windy days in June, two failed. On the two remaining, some birds managed to hatch eggs but by mid-July, both had been abandoned, with no chicks reaching fledgling age. The terns that swooped above my head as a child no longer return to the Outrun.

Arctic skuas and great skuas (bonxies) also nest on the hill. The skuas practise kleptoparasitism, harassing gulls and other birds to drop their food which they then claim. Unlike in other places, bonxies are a common sight here: Orkney and Shetland have 60 per cent of the global population. On the North Hill, twenty-two pairs of Arctic skuas were counted last year, down from forty-four in 2010.

Over the last twenty years, the number of seabirds around

Scottish coasts has dramatically declined. Like all the cliff colonies in Orkney, Fowl Craig is not as busy as it was during my childhood. The main reason for the decline is changes to the birds' food supply. The temperature of the North Sea has increased by around one degree centigrade in the past twenty-five years and there has been a drop in the amount of plankton, and in turn sand eels, which feed on plankton. This has meant problems for the seabirds whose primary food is sand eels: Arctic terns, kittiwakes, guillemots and shags. Without enough sand eels, the terns lose strength and have to travel further to find food. They may fail to nest, or if they do, they may be unable to find enough food for themselves and their chicks.

The great auk, now extinct, was a relative of the razorbill and stood about a metre high. The last breeding great auk in Britain was shot in 1813 on Papay, ordered by a collector in London. In the nineties, Papay schoolkids performed a play about the bird: *Raiders of the Last Auk*. I take a picture of the sea arch at Fowl Craig, and when I look at it on my computer, I see that my shadow has been cast on the cliff, standing on a ledge, squat and inadvertently looking like a lonely great auk, two hundred years after its death.

But while some species are failing, others are doing well. The North Hill has one of the biggest colonies of Scottish primrose (*Primula scotica*) in the world. These special flowers only grow to about four centimetres, with the flowers about eight millimetres in diameter, and thrive in salty, wind-lashed environments where other flowers can't. They are found only in a few coastal areas in the north of Scotland and need specific conditions to survive, neither under- nor over-grazed. Every three years, a full count of every *Primula scotica* flower on the North Hill is undertaken and last summer the total count was 8,134. I counted 617, on my hands and knees crawling along roped-out lanes.

I help with a monthly winter survey of birds on Papay. The absence of trees helps in the count and I scan the hill and coastline with binoculars. There is a rainbow over the sea and I stop for a while to watch gannets dive. They fold their wings swiftly and efficiently to form a perfect arrow when entering the sea. Observing them, I have a sensory memory of the meteor shower a few weeks earlier: the darting descent in the corner of my eye, the flash or the splash at the end, the thrill. Unlike most seabirds, gannets have been one of the few recent success stories of breeding around Orkney. The colony at Noup Head on Westray, which only began in 2003 with three nesting pairs, has grown to 623 nests.

On a Monday morning in mid-January, on our small island, 47 species of bird are counted including 102 curlew, 280 purple sandpiper, 276 fulmar, 16 red-breasted merganser, 1,000 starling, two hen harriers, one kestrel and 1,500 greylag geese. There are many hundreds of birds for each human resident.

Fowl Flag is the most northerly part of the whole island, a treacherous acre or so wedge of blue-black flagstone, sloping into the crashing waves, carpeted with slidy black lichen. I see lichen's photobiology played out on the rocks: black/green in areas that are damp, white/grey in the dry and yellow in 'splash areas'.

Around Fowl Flag, marked on the map, there are caves. I lie on my front on the cliff edge, trying to stick my head out far enough to glimpse one. The best way to see the caves is from the sea. Fisherman Douglas tells me that he has taken a boat inside some of the caves, which can extend back fifty metres into the island, and that you can go into one cave and come out of another. The hill is riddled and the ground beneath my feet is hollow.

I develop a walk, straight and compass drawn, up the spine of the island, past the telegraph-pole lookout to the trig point on North Hill. When I turn at the top of the hill to look back over the island, the diffuse winter sun shines from the south straight up the road. It's windy today and the sun has struggled to break through the haar. The island is hazy and trembling.

In the mist I hallucinate. I transpose the island's boundaries onto a map of London. Papay is about half the area of Hackney but has just a hundred-thousandth of the population. In my dream state the central road through Papay becomes Mare Street, the same north–south drag, and in each field springs a block of buildings. The Holm is the marshes and the loch is the park, the power lines are train tracks, each house a station. The screaming gulls become sirens, and the sea is traffic.

I once cycled along a Hackney towpath in winter, through fog so thick and cold that, when I emerged, frozen droplets of water were caught in my eyelashes.

★　　★　　★

One morning I'm out walking on the hill when there is some unexpected sunshine. I'm striding on in sudden good spirits when the thought pings into my head that the thing to complete this mood would be a cold pint of beer. It gets me at my worst times but also in my best moments. I'm crying. I'm sober, twenty months and eight days now, and I like the changes happening in my life but I'm still often frustrated about not being 'able' to drink. I'm sober but I would like a drink. It's a painful paradox to live in.

For a while after I stopped drinking I was on a drug called Campral, prescribed to help with the cravings. But no medication is going to eradicate the deeper thirst. It's not that I want the alcohol itself, it's that I want to feel the effects it gave me: I want to feel easier. My problem is not physical. And even if I did get rid of the cravings, I am still left with the question of why I had that need in the first place – and what will fill the void.

In defiance of this dissatisfaction, I'm conducting my own form of therapy through long walks, cold swims and methodically reading old journals. I'm learning to identify and savour freedom: freedom of place, freedom from damaging compulsion. I'm filling the void with new knowledge and moments of beauty. The dangerous thoughts will happen – and while I'm experiencing them I feel like that's the way I will feel for ever – but I just have to let the cravings pass lightly. I must not entertain them and help them to grow.

On a windy day, I climb and kneel unsteadily on top of the trig point on North Hill. Sunlight is making a rainbow through sea spray. I then continue right out to Fowl Flag. On the clifftop my heart is wild and open and empty. I've reached the edge. I howl as loudly as I can into the churning Bore, my cry caught by the waves and blown back to the shore, into the inaccessible caves, echoing and rumbling deep below my feet.

19

ONLINE

WHEN I ARRIVED AT ROSE Cottage, I made sure broadband was working before the hot water. I'm medieval with Wi-Fi: concentrating on the fundamentals of making fire and baking bread while becoming increasingly reliant on my smartphone.

Wherever I am, I spend most of my time with a laptop online, so I might as well do it in the calm and beautiful surroundings of Papay. In the past decade or so, the internet has made island life possible for more people, able to work remotely for employers down south. This way of working increases hope that the fragile populations of some of the smaller islands will not only stabilise but grow. The internet can be more important to remote communities than it is in cities. Since I've been sober and in Orkney, I'm online more than ever as a way of keeping myself linked to the old life I'm not prepared to cut ties with. I'm keeping in spectral communication with the ghosts of my past.

There can be connection problems. Our internet on Papay comes through the copper phone lines as the population size does not justify the phone companies installing fibre-optic cables. The signal is sent by microwaves from Kirkwall to Shapinsay to Sanday to Westray then to us, declining in speed with each transition. The mobile signal can be affected by the wind, and one side of the island gets the Orange signal, the other O2. I'm waiting for the next gale to receive my text messages.

In the islands in the age of digital media, we often find that, although it seems contradictory, technology can bring us closer to the wild. When an unusual bird, such as a sea eagle, is seen in the sky above Orkney, or a pod of orca along the coastline, people pass messages immediately via a local birding forum or text-message groups so that others can rush out to see them. Alerts on the possibilities of seeing the Merry Dancers circulate on the social networks and, the next day or the same night, people share their photographs.

On Sanday, a webcam is trained on the colony of grey seals that pup in November. I post a link on Facebook and my friends in offices in London watch the hulking grey females hauled up on the beach with their white teddy-bear-like pups, unable to swim yet. We chat while watching seals caught before dawn by night-vision camera and a black-backed gull eating a seal's afterbirth.

I think of Maggie and her lifelong connection to a place; her memories of names and houses on the island were similar to the way I can place people I know to different corners and times of the internet. Many of them I've never met in person but we've vaguely followed each other's lives for years. Often I feel as if my real life is inside the computer while my time back in Orkney and the people I see here are just a temporary intrusion. I know people on Twitter I've never met better than people I've sat opposite for months at work or people I went to school with. I've moved around a lot but the internet is my home.

I begin to use a GPS app on my phone to track my daily walks around Papay, along sheep trails and high-water lines. I'm building a map, within the limits of the island, revealing the lines I am drawn along. Overlaid on satellite maps, a story emerges. The GPS tracks show how my walks change. At first I stride out, covering good distances along the coastal paths, marking my territory. As the weeks go on, I become slower and more exploratory, covering smaller areas in greater detail: climbing down the stones into a geo, looking in rockpools for treasures.

Cross-referencing the shoreline with the Ordnance Survey map in my pocket, Google Maps on my phone and my physical and visual experience, I am locating myself, putting the correct names to the inlets and outcrops around the North Hill. The Pow of Keldie looks like a potential spot to swim at low tide; Mad Geo is dark and intense. For me, these places – 'The Sneck', 'Eerival' – exist both digitally and underfoot.

Orkney and Shetland often used to appear in a box at the side of the map, to the east of Britain rather than the north. Now Google Maps stretches endlessly around the globe. Late at night, I keep ending up on the Wikipedia page for and satellite view of Sule Skerry, to the west of the Outrun, just beyond the horizon, home in the spring to thousands of breeding puffins and gannets. It seems the tides are strong around these parts of the internet, pushing me back here again and again.

With the Sky Map app, I am able to point my phone at the night sky and name which stars and planets are in that direction. One night, a friend asks me what that bright star is, and when I answer that I think it's not a star but Jupiter, the app confirms that I am correct, improving my confidence in my meagre astronomy knowledge. The programme marks the horizon, like a spirit level, providing a digital gravity even on the windiest, darkest night. Down there, on the other side of the world, is the International Space Station, only visible to people in the southern hemisphere tonight. Astronauts on-board tweet photographs of their view back to us on earth and people reply with long-exposure images they took of the station passing above, a trail of light across the continents.

One morning, I have a tip-off on Facebook that orca have been seen hunting dolphins along the west coast of Orkney, heading north. I go out to the North Hill and look for them. I am all eyes, my body efficiently insulated. I don't see any whales but I watch a huge ship just disappearing from view. I think it must be an oil tanker heading out to one of the North Sea oil platforms but, back at the cottage, I look on the marine-traffic website and find that she is Russian cargo ship *Kuzma Minin*, with a destination of Kandalaksha in northern Russia. The flight-radar website tells me that the contrail high above Westray one clear dawn is the overnight Lufthansa flight from Los Angeles to Frankfurt.

The more I take the time to look at things, the more rewards and complexity I find. Long-exposure photographs glow super-naturally. With all these tabs open on my browser, I feel omniscient, watching how global-transport logistics dance and intersect, never crashing, like flocks of starling.

Seabirds have been caught and fitted with satellite tracking devices, GPS data loggers, finding out, often for the first time, just how far they travel searching for food. One fulmar tagged by Yvan and Juliet on Copinsay was found to have flown as far as Norway before returning to its nest. The corncrakes were tracked to Africa with daylight geolocators, which stopped working when they finished their migration and again found shelter in long foliage, blocking exposure to the daylight. While kayaking this summer, Mum saw a basking shark in Scapa Flow, anecdotally a species increasing in numbers in our seas. Aiming to quantify these stories, researchers have fitted twenty basking sharks on the west coast of Scotland with trackers and we are able to watch their movements in close-to-real time on the internet.

I am not tracking a mysterious or endangered species: I am carrying out semi-scientific studies into myself, performing bathymetry of the soul. My last.fm counts every song I listen to, constantly updating lists of my favourite artists and recommending new ones. My Facebook prioritises the friends I interact with. I jostle for retweets and edgerank. I am in an ever-changing process of defining myself, fascinated by counting and plotting and marking my daily activities and movements, collecting bottomless data. I've been tracking my sleep cycles and carrying out surveys of my dreams. I download a menstrual-cycle recorder and watch it sync with the moon, waxing and waning in another window on my browser.

With my phone, I record the noise of the wind and rain on my Rose Cottage bedroom window late one night during a gale. According to my dosimeter – the noise-measuring app on my phone – the sound of the weather is averaging 68 decibels from my bed, about the level of a loud conversation, making it hard to sleep. I remember these noises from my childhood bedroom at the farm. I remember shouting into ears in night-clubs, trying to be heard above the music. Tonight the wind and my phone are my companions.

I record the sound of the breaking waves at Fowl Craig, the greylag geese that sometimes mysteriously honk and rise late at night, wind in the telegraph wires and the familiar hum of the propeller plane. I upload my recordings to the internet – twenty-second sensory postings from my island life, like poems.

Sometimes, though, the internet – all this hyper-connection – just makes me lonelier. Chatting on Skype, looking at the screen rather than the camera, creates a shifty dissociation, a not-quite eye-contact. Meeting in real life, we are unsure, blinking and leaving too long before responses. We spend too much time online and real life is just another window. What's the point in going out to look at wildlife when I can watch nature documentaries on YouTube, in bed with an electric blanket?

I half wake in the night with rootless anxiety and grasp for my phone. The internet is still a place I turn to for comfort and I used to post online when I had been drinking. Lately, I have been tidying up trails I left in different parts of the internet under multiple identities, some years ago, while drunk. I used to spill my heart over the internet like red wine.

'Cross-addiction' is the idea that, in the absence of drink, alcoholics will transfer their addictive behaviour to something else. It's commonly seen with food, exercise, shopping or gambling. For me, it's Coca-Cola, smoking, relationships and the internet. Sometimes I am smoking one cigarette while craving the next. I can fixate on a new friend and escape into their internet profiles, wanting to obliterate my personality with theirs.

There's an emptiness. I've lost booze and I am desperately searching for what I need to fill me up. Is it coffee, sex, writing, love, new clothes or online approval? I read about how these beeps and notifications and vibrations affect and alter our brains, giving small jolts of dopamine, a little adrenaline. Searching for that tiny buzz, I am circling round familiar websites, like a migrating bird following rivers or motorways. The red notification of a message I've been waiting for gives a shadow of the sensation of the first sip of beer, of cold water when you're parched, of a soft bed when you're exhausted, of giving up swimming when you're ready to drown.

I have twenty tabs open, each an endless journey, an unfinished thought. I can't go to sleep yet: there are too many tabs open in my brain. This thirst feels unquenchable. I read old emails dozens of times, trying to find something that's not there any more. I'm trying to find the right thing to fill this hole but it always eludes me, just at the brink of my consciousness, the corner of my eye, the thing you went to pick up but then found you couldn't remember what it was – the island just over the horizon.

In this emptiness, I miss alcohol. I miss drink like I missed my boyfriend. I begin to think that maybe AA is like the fundamentalist Christian camps in the US where gay people try to become straight. Maybe it is cruel and unnatural to force me from my path as an alcoholic. I don't remember excessive drinking in our house when I was a child, although I know that Dad drank more when he was high. As soon as I started drinking as a teenager, though, I did so with a dangerous urgency. The pieces were already in place for me to be a drinker and now it hurts to be made to do otherwise.

At least alcohol gives a quantifiable answer to the non-specific question: it fills a void. Without it, I am left to figure out what the question was – and that's where AA suggests that its 12 Step Programme comes in. Step One: 'We admitted we were powerless over alcohol – that our lives had become unmanageable.' I had done this some time ago, when I went into the treatment centre, but I have been reluctant to undertake the rest.

My time in treatment taught me to recognise feelings and to try to understand what certain types of behaviour are trying to achieve and what they actually will. I take a step back from my blank-minded mouse-clicking and notice how, when my phone runs out of batteries, I can almost feel I don't exist, my walk no longer being tracked. I want to be able to use all this technology for its benefits but keep it under control, not be sucked under. I'm aware of my addictive and obsessive tendencies.

I'm using technology to take myself to the centre of something from my spot at the edge of the ocean. I'm trying to make sense of my environment. With my digital devices, the planes and birds and stars seem more quantifiable and trackable. I'm trying to make a connection with the world outside Papay and my old life. I take a photograph of the sun setting over Westray and upload it to Facebook. My sky is converted into zeroes and ones, my personal data beamed to satellites, bounced through fibre-optic cables under the sea, through microwaves and copper wire, over islands, to you.

20

SEA SWIMMING

I N THE FIRST WEEKS OF our relationship, he was still charmed by the spontaneous, drunken aspects of my character that later drove us apart. Late one night we boosted and pulled each other over the ten-foot walls of the inner London lido near where I lived back then – we found scratches and bruises the next day – and dropped silently onto the tiled poolside. The water was luxuriously warm in the cold night and we swam a couple of lengths, under moonlight and CCTV, naked but for balaclavas. I still have some photos, the flash bright on our pale skin.

I've sought the thrill of swimming outdoors once again now I'm back in Orkney. I joined an eccentric group called the Orkney Polar Bears who, every Saturday morning year-round, go swimming in the sea at a different location around the islands.

I prepare by eating porridge and listening to aggressive rap. We make a strange group: undressing car-side into swimming costumes, woolly hats and goose-bumps. Going sea swimming with a group provides the motivation that is lacking when you're alone. Everyone has different techniques for getting into the water – some running enthusiastically, others repeatedly edging up to genital level before backing out.

The swims are a way to experience the changing seasons and different parts of Orkney, location decided following analysis of the tides and wind direction. The nature of islands means that even a relatively small place has miles of coastline, often new to me and empty. We've swum at a bridge beside the main road, where we were beeped at by passing lorries; at a secluded sandy beach reached by a drive down a long, pot-holed track and climbing over fences, getting stung by nettles; in rockpools; in the harbour.

We often swim to shipwrecks, the Second World War block-ships that lie around Orkney's coast; up close their rusting hulls loom above us. We see the land from a different perspective and have encounters with birds: I once swam right up to a tystie and have had Arctic terns diving nearby.

It's different from swimming in a heated, chlorinated, right-angled pool. Sometimes curious seals come close and swim with us. A swimmer friend dived under and pulled up a handful of clams that she took home and cooked for lunch. We swim over sand, over pebbles, over seaweed and silt, with the birds and fish, in all weathers.

We swim in windscreen-wipers-on-highest-setting rain when we rush to get into the water where it's dryer. We're lifted by the bow waves of passing boats. The water is always different:

sometimes dark and velvety, sometimes perfectly clear, flat and glassy. We swim when sunshine dapples the surface and illuminates bubbles under water.

On 1 May, in celebration of May Day or Beltane, we meet at dawn – five fourteen a.m. – at the most easterly beach on the Orkney Mainland, where we can see the sun rise over the ocean horizon. The sea is black and thick when we walk in, but as the sun rises, it lights our laughing, yelping faces and catches the rippling waves.

We swim on the minute of the summer solstice at the north coast of the Mainland, just after midnight at 12:09 a.m. when it is still light in the grimlins. The next morning I smell of bonfire smoke and taste of sea salt. Following the points of the compass and the turning points of the year, we go to the west coast for sunset on Lammas, an ancient celebration of the first harvest. It's a misty night with no sunset and it's spooky in the geo, where we slip on seaweed and my fellow swimmers are half shrouded in the fog. I was on Papay when the group swam after dark on the winter solstice, wearing head torches, guided back to the shore by a light on the beach. It feels ritualistic, this celebration of solstices and equinoxes, following compass points, moon and tide charts and sunrise calendars.

I didn't realise until I was back in Orkney and more aware of these things, but the day after my last drink – my first day sober – was the spring equinox, 20 March. Since then, each solstice and equinox has marked another quarter-year of sobriety. I enjoy this: it links my small choices and individual behaviour into the patterns of the solar system. The swims are a way to celebrate.

It is always gaspingly cold. The sea temperature gets gradually higher all summer, to an average of a 'cold' thirteen degrees in September; then, when the air temperature becomes cooler than the water, it goes down to an 'extremely cold' four or so degrees in February. The first time felt like it was burning my skin but each Saturday it gets slightly easier – your body acclimatises – although I am the wimpiest member of the club, back onshore drying myself while the others are still breast-stroking around the pier. It's a convivial group, heads up, chatting while we swim.

I want to shock myself awake: after central heating and screens, to feel cold, with skin submerged in wild waters, is attractively physical. I want to blast away the frustrations of being stuck on this island and no longer have the outlet of getting drunk. The chilly immersion is addictive, verging on unpleasant at the time, but I find myself craving it, agreeing to go again, planning my next swim, eyeing up lochs, bays or reservoirs. I want to swim in bomb craters.

During each of the first few swims there is a point when my body panics. I picture drowning and, knowing the depth beneath me, my heart rate increases. I need to reach the shore as quickly as possible. When I do pull myself out up the slipway, climbing the ladder onto the pier, or washing up with the waves onto the beach, I feel saved: reborn and very alive.

People claim all sorts of health benefits from wild swimming – better circulation, improved immunity – with the Outdoor Swimming Society pledging to 'embrace the rejuvenating effects of cold water' but I mainly do it for the 'cold-water high', the exhilaration and endorphins resulting from even a short dip.

Afterwards, I go about my Saturday – first stop the supermarket – with a crazy smile and bright red salty skin. Other Polar Bears report an increase of energy to start the weekend but one member told me she just enjoys that other people think she's mad. It's an unconventional hobby and a weekly adventure.

When I move to Papay, I decide to swim on Saturdays at ten a.m., the same time as the Mainland Polar Bears: the club's solo outpost member. I cycle the five hundred metres down to the bay at North Wick, drop my bike on the sand dunes, strip and run into the morning sun on turquoise water. The sea at North and South Wick is always a vivid aquamarine, due to its clarity, shallowness and the sand underneath, but the tropical colour belies its chill.

As I take my clothes off and leave them on the shore, I remember stripping in a stranger's flat in London. I remember that frustration and anger. This is all I've got. This is what you have reduced me to. I am not in so much pain today but I am the same person: naked and raw.

There are things about the sea you find out only by being in it. The waves carry stones, large pebbles suspended in the water, thrown around effortlessly. I watch, from a seal's-eye perspective, a gull descend and land on the water. It seems not to have noticed me. One morning, the sky is reflected in the flat water and I'm swimming in the clouds.

I miss the encouragement of the group when I swim alone.

One chilly Saturday morning, I cycle down to the beach, look at the waves for a while, take off my breeks and feel the cold north wind, drizzle and sea spray on my legs, but just can't bring myself to get into the water. I've found my limit.

Seals pop up their heads close by when we swim, interested in our human presence, looking at us with familiar eyes. We are mirror images, both at the edge of our worlds, only able to share a small proportion of our territory. On my walks, I'm sure it is the same pair following me around the island. One watches me so intently that it seems the sea takes it by surprise and I watch, through the clear water, its body flail, suspended in a breaking wave.

I'm not the first person to think a seal is my friend. 'Selkie' is the Orcadian word for 'seal' but it also has links to the tales of seals shifting into human form. Selkies, it is said, slip from their seal skins as beautiful naked people, who dance on beaches under the moon, as described by George Mackay Brown in *Beside the Ocean of Time*: 'And there on the sand, glimmering, were men and women – strangers – dancing! And the rocks were strewn with seal skins!' If the seal skin was lost or stolen, the selkies would be unable to transform back. There are stories of men hiding skins and taking a seal-maiden as a wife, but she would always belong in the sea.

Some say the selkie idea was invented by lonely sailors as an excuse for falling for the mournful song of a seal but there were many who believed. In the 1890s a mermaid was seen in Deerness in the East Mainland 'with hundreds of eyewitnesses swearing to the validity of their encounters'.

By swimming in the sea I cross the normal boundaries. I'm no longer on land but part of the body of water making up all the oceans of the world, which moves, ebbing and flowing under and around me. Naked on the beach, I am a selkie slipped from its skin.

I have a quote written in my diary but I can't find the source: 'Swim naked whenever you can, summer or winter, you'll never die.' Swimming has long been prescribed as tonic or cure. After my swims on Papay I get into the shower, balancing the stimulation of cold water with soothing heat. I am performing my own method of hydrotherapy, historically used in the treatment of alcoholics, often against their will. AA founder Bill W was treated with hydrotherapy for alcoholism in the early 1930s. Alcoholic and mentally ill actress Frances Farmer, incarcerated, was put in cages with other madwomen and sprayed with hot and cold water.

Mum's church performs baptisms on the beaches of Orkney. Two elders walk with the new convert into the cold sea and, holding an arm each, plunge them under the waves, symbolising their new birth as followers of Jesus. They come back smiling and shivering in wet clothes to what they hope is life anew. The cold water is cathartic. It's refreshing, like the first drink; it offers transformation and escape, like intoxication, like drowning. I am so thirsty and full of desire.

Once after being out all night at a party in a squatted east London warehouse, Gloria and I decided, high and wide-eyed, that what we needed was a dawn swim in Hampstead Heath ladies' pond. We had grimy rave skin and sleep deprivation and thought the cold water would provide refreshment and even salvation. The sun was coming up and the tube reopening as we made our way north. Down at the pond we met a group of elderly women and one told us that she swims in the outdoor natural pool every morning of the year, that it is her health and happiness.

Lately, I've noticed a gradual reprogramming. In the past when I was under stress, my first impulse was to drink, to get into the pub or the off-licence. A house-moving day years ago once ended a month-long attempt at sobriety. Now, sometimes, I'm not just fighting against these urges but have developed new ones. Even back in the summer, set free after a frustrating day in the RSPB office, my first thought was sometimes not a pint but 'Get in the sea.' Swimming shakes out my tension and provides refreshment and change. I am finding new priorities and pleasures for my free time. I've known this was possible but it takes a while for emotions to catch up with intellect. I am getting stronger.

The motivation is the same but my methods of dealing with the way I feel are changing. I used to confuse my neurotransmitters on a Friday night in a hot nightclub. Now I shock my senses on a Saturday morning in a biting sea, plunging warm skin into cold water, forcing a rush of sensation, cleansed.

21

THE HOLM

O N GOOGLE MAPS, LOOKING AT uninhabited island the Holm of Papay, the satellite picture gives way to the default cerulean ocean blue. The Holm is where the internet ends, beyond the realm of digital cartographers: here be cyber monsters.

Britain is an island off Europe, Orkney is an island off Britain, Westray is an island off Orkney, Papay is an island off Westray and the Holm of Papay is at yet another remove. It is where to go when life on Papay gets too hectic.

There are 'holms' (pronounced 'homes') all around Orkney, the name coming from the Old Norse word *hólmr* meaning 'small island', offshore islets near the coast of a bigger island. The Holm of Papay is our 'calf' island, constantly in view to the east, a wedge shape topped by a stone cairn, across just a few hundred metres of shallow azure water. At low tide rocks are exposed between the two islands, and when people lived at the Knap of Howar, more than five thousand years ago, they might have been joined by land.

On a calm, bright morning, Neil, the farmer at Holland – the farm in the centre of Papay, seat of the island's lairds from the seventeenth to the nineteenth century – rings to tell me they will be taking a ram over to the Holm and I can come along. I career down to the old pier on my bike.

The ram, small and horned, is manhandled from a trailer into a little boat. He will have just a few weeks to carry out his one job of the year: servicing about twenty of the ewes on the Holm selected to have lambs in the spring. The crossing, in a small boat with four people, a ram and a sheepdog, takes less than ten minutes. Today, without much wind, I can see right to the bottom of the seabed: the water is clear, the surface unruffled.

Stepping off the boat onto an island where we are the only humans, I get a sense, as I did on Copinsay, of exhilaration tinged with fear. The birds and seals seem bigger and tougher. I take a wide berth around a fulmar in case it tries to vomit on me. There are hidden geos, pointed away towards North Ronaldsay, their secrets seen only by occasional visitors or from the sea. There is a dead seal pup on the grass by the shore but when I get closer it moves and I realise it is not dead at all but basking in the rare winter sun. Eighty or so 'holmie' ewes stay on the Holm all year round and, especially in the winter when the grass is scarce, live off a diet that includes seaweed. These sheep are incredibly hardy to survive out here all winter without extra food. The similar hill breeds we used to have on the farm were my favourite, more nimble-footed and independent than the stocky, docile Texels or Suffolks. The odd ewe would develop an ability to jump fences, breaking free of the nursery fields onto the Outrun, and was sometimes followed, squeezing through the barbed wire, by her lambs. Once a year in summer on Papay, there is 'holmie day', one of the last remnants of communal farming in Orkney, when islanders go over to the Holm to help to catch and shear the sheep.

There are no signs that the Holm has ever been inhabited yet it is where the ancient people brought their dead. There are three chambered tombs, the biggest of which, the south cairn, well excavated and maintained, is now looked after by Historic Scotland. Due to its inaccessibility, it is Historic Scotland's least visited site.

I see the cairn every day from Rose Cottage and it is strange now to be standing on top of it, the low sun casting my shadow over the island. I lift a metal hatch and descend a ladder into the mound. I use the torch left for visitors to crawl through the long passageway and look into the ten small cells or enclosures leading off. There are carvings of what look like eyebrows on the stone, similar to the 'eyes' of the Westray Wife.

A friend tells me that the cairn is – like the tomb of Maeshowe on the Orkney Mainland – aligned with the midwinter sun. At Maeshowe, on the solstice and a few days on either side, on the rare cloudless days at that time of year, the setting sun will shine directly down the entrance corridor. Webcams are set up there and one midwinter afternoon I watch over the internet as the golden light hits the end wall.

I had a reckless idea to get farmer Neil or fisherman Douglas to take me out to the Holm one day around midwinter and leave me overnight – for both sunset and sunrise – so I could investigate and find out if there is any sun alignment. I thought I was brave and had no superstitions to stop me spending a night in the tomb, but now, after just a few minutes down there, I want to get out: it is cold, damp, dark and scary. There is no way I'm going to spend a night there.

I climb out of the cairn and walk to the south-east corner of the Holm, the part that is not on Google Maps, and feel I have escaped. I am beyond the internet.

I am attracted to these places at the edge. I crave either life in the inner city or to go to islands beyond islands, islands of the dead. In a Hackney pub Gloria and I played pool with two guys who invited us back to their place across the road where they had some beers. Their place was a homeless hostel. A few nights later we were in a luxury hotel with a band, sneaking into the sauna in the early hours, spraying each other's warm skin with plastic bottles of cold water until the fridge was empty. I want to have splendid success or to fail beautifully.

Sometimes I'm indignant: it's unjust that a conscientious person such as me, with much good fortune, opportunity and support, ended up in rehab. But when I look at it from another perspective, it's no surprise at all. Extremes were normal for me. I grew up with mental illness: unpredictable flurries of unusual and wild behaviour, followed by withdrawn lows. I remember in glimpses: looking up at Dad and Mum fighting and pushing at the top of the stairs, a neighbour taking me out of the house, and when I came back Dad being gone for weeks or months. I was born into dramatic scenes, lived in the landscape of shipwrecks and howling storms, with animal birth and death, religious visions, on the edge of chaos, with the possibility of something exciting happening at the same time as the threat of something going wrong. A part of me thinks that these wildly swinging fluctuations are, if not normal, at least desirable, and I grew to expect and even seek the edge. The alternative, of balance, seems pale and limited. I seek sensation and want to be more alive.

At the edge of the Holm, I spin around on the spot for a few rotations – the islands on the horizon whirl around me in a blurred panorama. I'm dipping in and out of phone reception and satellite view, trying to get one step ahead of my short attention span, spinning like the rotating beams when I slept at the bottom of the lighthouse or the helicopter's blades on the day I was born.

I don't have long here before Neil wants to go back to Papay – lighter without the ram – and get on with the rest of the day's work, so I make my way across the Holm to the boat. Gradually, on winter walks and these exploratory trips, my understanding of myself is growing. I'm seeing patterns and tracing the roots of my desires. But in order to find a way forward, I will need help.

I first encountered Dee when she emailed offering her support as another sober woman in Orkney. At that point I didn't know that I would be coming to live on her island: she and her husband, Mo, had moved to Papay four years ago and since then had turned a derelict croft into a warm home. I had not asked anyone to be my sponsor. I was only interested in someone who shared my prejudices and didn't mention Jesus.

Before I went to my first AA meeting, four or five years before my time in the treatment centre, I spent a long time reading material on the internet that criticised the organisation: alternative programmes that allowed you to drink in moderation and articles on atheist fora. I was suspicious of the coercive and religious aspects of the programme, wanted to be fully informed and, if possible, have an excuse not to attend.

The essential paradox of AA/NA, and the treatment centre, is that the thing we are trying to eradicate from our lives – the thing we used obsessively to seek out and consume – is the very thing we spend all day discussing, analysing, reminiscing about. Many would say that it is simply replacing one way of being fixated with it for another.

When I'm in a spiky mood I fear it will be impossible ever to leave the world of addiction, that I'll be defined by alcohol – or, more accurately, *defined by its absence* – for ever. I don't want to be endlessly telling the newcomers about what I took, what it made me do and how I kicked it. I want to do other things with my liberation.

Back in the treatment centre, I was sometimes scared about what the treatment programme was turning me into. Endlessly self-absorbed and self-doubting, I was shocked to find myself speaking platitudes that used to make my brain recoil. Was my moral compass wonky? We listened to people 'share' about terrible behaviour and crimes they had committed under the influence, and praised them for being 'honest'. I hung out all day with jailbirds, junkies and crackheads, and nodded when one peer told me proudly that his family was so well connected in Bangladesh that his brother had literally got away with murder.

I had a lot of prejudice against AA: that it would in some way brainwash me, that I would have to relinquish intellectual control; that if I was in an AA meeting on a Saturday morning then I might just as well be in a church on a Sunday morning; that the 'Big Book' is really a Bible; that I would start using recovery-therapy jargon in everyday speech – 'resentments', 'taking inventory', 'relapse', 'the rooms', 'dry drunk', 'higher power'.

But around me, in meetings, I heard people who said they were atheists and used the programme, people who seemed to have maintained their personality, sense of humour and critical thought, people who were doing things with their lives. An AA friend gave me a useful way of seeing the jargon as a kind of internal 'Esperanto' – a way of shorthanding complex ideas and experiences so we know what we're talking to each other about.

I have been – successfully – working the first parts of the programme. Not having a drink one day – one hour, one minute – at a time, but failing to move beyond that into acceptance of and contentment in my new sober state. While I have doubts about AA, I have been struggling and need help so am willing to give it a try.

It seems fortuitous to be on a tiny island with a woman who has decades of sobriety behind her so I, nervously, ask Dee to take me through the 12 Steps during my time on Papay. We begin with a study of AA's Big Book. I can't decide whether I'm taking control or letting go.

★   ★   ★

On midwinter days the sky never gets beyond murky, but at what could be called dusk I walk down the coast in keen wind and hard rain to the Knap of Howar. I shelter down by the Stone Age structure and admire – one dyke-builder to another – the curved walls that have stood for five thousand years. I imagine living here. Like Rose Cottage, it has a hearth, and it has a stone for crushing seeds and making bread. I could be cosy under a whale-ribs roof, covered with animal skins.

Although the sun is obscured by grey stratus cloud, I feel I should come down here for sunset on the solstice – when the passageway at Maeshowe is aligned – to somehow mark and celebrate another quarter-year sober. I feel a bit silly waiting for something to happen but at 15:15, exactly sunset, across the water of Papa Sound, which is being blown against the tide by the wind in trembling ripples, the landing lights at the airstrip on Westray pop on: eight bright stars in the murk.

From inside the roofless Stone Age house, I watch the plane hop over from Westray, two white wing-lights and one red tail-light, guided into the Papay airfield by the runway lights, a new installation meaning that flights can be extended later into winter nights. People come from far afield to wonder at our ancient monuments but these are our daily miracles. My Neolithic fantasy may be broken but I am in a new awe: of the transport system, skilful pilots guiding the planes, in the strongest winds, down at midwinter to the lights of home.

22

PERSONAL GEOLOGY

I've been trying to remember my last drink, almost two years ago, the weekend before I started the detox programme. It must have been the dregs of someone else's, picked up at the end of the night in a pub in south London as I stumbled around desperately. I then got into a taxi I couldn't afford and, at traffic lights near my house, opened the door, ran and hid from the driver in the walkways of a Bethnal Green estate, heart pounding. That hadn't been my plan for the evening. It never was.

The Big Book describes well the vicious cycle of 'the Alcoholic': the drunken sprees, after which 'coming to his senses, he [the drunk] is revolted at certain episodes he vaguely remembers', how the memories are pushed away, and how the alcoholic lives in fear and tension that lead to more drinking.

There were secrets of the night. Wonderful and dreadful things happened, I met and re-met people, but in the sober daylight, at work, it seemed impossible that that was me. At times, I liked this dangerous part of myself but I knew the game was up when I began drinking to ease the memories of the night before. Lonely and despairing, I was lost in what the Book calls 'that bitter morass of self-pity'. I was sinking and knew that alcohol had beaten me.

Walking around the island, it is hard to not start thinking about how the land itself was formed. Even a short stretch of coast has a variety of interesting rock formations: precarious piles of parallelograms where rockpools gather, parts that look like 'crazy paving', undulating ripples like waves. Layers of rock are clearly visible on the cliffs, like the pages of a book. These layers on different islands once met up when the archipelago was one continuous landmass but have been worn away by the action of sea and ice over millennia. Sea arches, sea stacks and caves are evidence of the continuing erosion.

Most of Orkney is formed from Caithness flagstone, grey sedimentary rock, locally called slate, dating back to the Devonian period 400 million years ago. It breaks in flat segments good for dyke-building. Some areas – in Hoy and Eday – are Orkney sandstone, the red stone that built St Magnus Cathedral in Kirkwall.

When sea levels stabilised after the last ice age, the islands of Orkney looked much as they do today but lacked detail. Over thousands of years, the sea has sculpted the coastline. On the more sheltered shorelines there is a gentle landscape but the exposed westerly coasts take the full force of waves that have travelled across the Atlantic, creating sea stacks and towering cliffs such as those at St John's Head on Hoy, standing straight up 365 metres above the sea.

This pattern is shown in miniature on Papay, with slanted rock formations and severe geos on the Atlantic side (like those on the west-facing Outrun) and gentler bays on the east. It alarms me to realise that each of the islands is getting gradually smaller, eaten away by the sea.

On geological maps of Orkney, a division runs through Papay, through the area of Rose Cottage, splitting the North Hill, and during my time on the island I search for the fault line although I am not sure what it will look like.

I am questioning why I became an alcoholic. Perhaps I was born that way, physically. In AA meetings I'd heard people repeat the theory that alcoholics' bodies process alcohol unusually, that we have a build-up or overproduction of acetone, which the body uses to break down alcohol: we are allergic to the thing we crave. It's an appealingly easy explanation, no longer used by most medical professionals.

Alternatively, although as far as I know there have been no other alcoholics in my family, I could have a genetic tendency. I could blame mental illness: I've read that all types of anxiety disorder are more common in children of manic depressives. Or it could be something that happened. Adverse childhood experiences are linked to an increased risk of addiction. I could blame distressing experiences – my parents' divorce or adolescent heartbreaks. But I was irritated when pressed by counsellors to look to my childhood. Despite growing up with manic depression, I was always loved, I wasn't abused and didn't feel traumatised. I thought this was too easy – absolving myself of responsibility, putting blame on my parents, who did their best. I generally thought it was simply a habit that had got out of control: over years of systematic drinking I had worn my brakes down, like the action of waves on rock, so much that they could never be repaired.

I take a walk on the hill on a day when a south-east wind is whipping energetic waves around Fowl Craig. I sit to watch the sea and think about Dad. I've been finding him difficult lately. Although he's not seen a shrink in fifteen years or taken medication in ten, he's been slightly agitated, erratic and excitable in recent weeks, behaving in the way that makes people who've known him for a long time fear he's heading for a manic episode.

When I was a teenager, shortly before the last time he was sectioned, Dad gave me a blank cheque to go into town to buy something – a cordless phone, I think – which was fun but undercut with worry because I knew by then that reckless spending was a symptom of mania. There is a thin line between being impulsive and being dangerous. Grandiose thoughts and irresponsibility with money are exciting until they aren't.

Now, he's discovered Facebook, a great thing for isolated farmers but some of the stuff he posts – flirting with women, provocative statements to usually shy Orcadian farmers – embarrasses me. He's frustrated when other people don't comment or laugh. The Royal College of Physicians describes the beginning stage of mania as 'an extreme sense of well-being, optimism and energy' characterised by 'grandiose thoughts and behaviour' and a tendency to be 'irritated with other people who don't share optimistic outlook'. In this buoyant, gregarious state he finds other people uptight.

However, I am sympathetic. As a wave breaks, sending clumps of foam jolting in my direction, it strikes me that I know how he feels *because I used to feel like that when I was drinking*. Symptoms of mania are similar to drunkenness: feeling high and optimistic, racing thoughts, impaired judgement and impulsiveness, acting recklessly. At the beginning it can be fun – making communications and plans, being confident and saying cheeky things that get a reaction. I would be the person pulling the unwilling onto the dance-floor, arguing with a bouncer to let me into a club, telling my boyfriend that I'd not done anything wrong, I was just trying to have fun, push the boundaries, really live.

Something occurs to me that I've never thought of before: perhaps my drinking was in part an attempt to attain the manic states I'd experienced through my father. It seems so simple and, unlike many other explanations I'd been offered for my drinking, makes sense. The idea that I'm not mentally ill but was pursuing my own mania fits what I was searching for with alcohol and how I tried to make myself feel. In a way, my drunkenness was an attempt to emulate and even impress, although I didn't succeed, my dad: I was wild and free and alive.

In drinking I'd chase a vision for how people could relate more openly, wanting to reach the edges and taste extremes. But I wilfully ignored complaints and problems. For other people, the sober and the sane, this behaviour is annoying. They feel uncomfortable around you and unsure how you're going to act. You can't be dancing all the time.

Each binge-drinking session is a manic-depressive cycle in miniature. The excitement and elation tip over into uncontrollable dangerous behaviour. The next day's hangover is the inevitable depressive period that follows. Coming back some time later, you survey the damage and eroded relationships and make apologies and promises to control it better next time, lost in self-pity and self-obsession.

I stand up, alert, from my stone seat: I've made a break-through − stirred by the energy of the sea and the wind − in understanding my own behaviour. I didn't find it in a thera-pist's office, or by conscientiously working through the programme, or talking to Dee, but outdoors, watching the waves. I've been reading about fluid dynamics and the math-ematical criteria for a wave breaking, when the wave height is more than one-seventh of the wavelength. There are different types of breaking waves − spilling, plunging, collapsing, surging − but although they collapse in different manners, there is only so much height any wave can sustain before it comes crashing down.

★　　★　　★

I should have known my drinking was doomed when I began to experience 'freezes' or mini seizures, coming earlier and earlier into a binge session.

It began with a tension in the wrists, a warning. Then my elbows would freeze and I lifted my drink with stiff arms, like a robot. No matter how I felt, I *had* to lift my drink. I stubbed my cigarette with difficulty. Then I couldn't talk or swallow and was drooling. I had to bounce on my tiptoes and literally bash my body against a wall to smash the tension away, or I'd be stuck in a hunched shape, falling off my chair onto the carpet in the same seated stance. I tried to drag myself onto the sofa. This again. And I knew with certainty that I was trapped, bound irresistibly to the substance that hurt me and the shameful routine of drinking alone.

The freezes also happened when I was out among people, and I would pull my body stiff-legged to the bathroom where I locked the door with a clenched fist and bounced until I was loose enough to rejoin the party, as if freezing and drooling but continuing to drink were normal. I knew it was a warning but for a long time my only aim was to make it go away so I could make it happen again.

Since then, I have read about alcoholic neuropathy – nerve damage caused by alcohol and vitamin deficiency – but at the time, although I kept on drinking, I knew that drinking was beginning to damage my brain. The American writer David Foster Wallace, an addict, described the irony of substance addiction: that it 'suggests itself as solution to its own problem'. Willingly inducing these seizures was insane but I felt trapped.

★　　★　　★

On the hill, I found something that I thought could be the fault line, a faint rocky ridge – but in many ways it doesn't matter what the cause was or where the fault line started. What matters is that I recognise the problem, which AA neatly summarises in Step One's description of powerlessness and unmanageability. Then I need to be willing (Steps Two and Three) to deal with the symptoms and move into living a sober life (Steps Four to Twelve). Elimination of my drinking was just a beginning – it tackled the physical side – made sure I avoided the craving that began once I started drinking. My body detoxified and recovered a long time ago now but the emotional side – the obsession – is still there.

Step Two says we 'came to believe that a Power greater than ourselves could restore us to sanity'. Dee asks me, before our next session, to consider if I believe that there is a power greater than myself.

Reluctantly, I think about the forces that I have experienced living on the islands: the wind and the sea. I think of erosion and corrosion. The power of corrosion is a huge problem in Orkney, and on tiny Papay even more so, due to the sea salt, which blows across the island and can be scraped from windows after storms. Anything metal, such as cars and bikes, will quickly rust.

I think of the power of animal instinct, guiding the corncrakes to Africa and me to my lover's house, dead drunk, late at night. I think about entropy, the concept behind the inevitable decline from order to disorder. On the beach I find fragments of glass-ware, an ashtray perhaps, that have been in the sea so long they've become half pebble.

Despite my discomfort that the question might push me into the dubious areas of spirituality that I find hard to grasp, I decide that I can accept the existence of some 'powers greater than myself' – not God, just the things I've always known, the forces I've grown up with, strong enough to smash up ships and carve islands.

The 12 Step Programme says that, in order to recover, alcoholics have to change and we need to have what some call a 'spiritual experience' and what is also described as 'huge emotional displacements and rearrangements'. I think of the way the sea can change the land. These shifts – movements of sand and rock – are usually gradual but sometimes sudden and monumental. The morning after easterly gales and high tides, there is a step down to the beach that had not been there before. The sea has taken away tonnes of sand overnight. It may be washed up on another part of the shoreline or taken out to the ocean bed, forming new layers of rock that, when Papay is long gone, may become new islands.

After centuries of gradual erosion, one day, geologically in the very near future, the Stack o' Roo will fall into the sea, felled by the same processes that shaped it. But as erosion proceeds, new sea arches will be carved from the cliffs, which in turn become stacks, which are eventually undermined. The island is always getting smaller, the cliff being carved ever more intricately. Life is getting sadder but more interesting – all the injuries and hurts, like scars in the coastline, continually worn away.

★　★　★

On my winter walks in the mornings, and during nights in the cottage trembling in the weather, old ideas about who I am, how I got like this and where I need to be are shifting. Personalities are formed by persistent, repeated actions, by learned patterns of behaviour and subtle approvals. Parents unconsciously influence their children to be some version of themselves.

I'm thinking longer term, in geological time, doing just what I can each day and not putting it off because it won't be brilliant. I'm not going for quick excitement or instant gratification but thinking about other people's feelings and the consequences.

One shift that I allow myself is to admit that I do miss the brief hours of intoxication and that it is a shame I can't toast someone's special occasion with champagne, share a bottle of wine with a man or enjoy a cold pint after work. I'm allowed to feel loss. But these losses are very small compared to the ability to keep a job or a relationship or some kind of sustainable stable state of mind. In any case, I have learned to model the process forward to what would happen if I did drink: chaos followed by depression.

Drinking alcoholically is an incomplete remedy, a repeated mistake, a journey that never reaches its destination. Whatever ease or high it did promise I could no longer reach: it ran away from me, always just over the horizon, like Hether Blether. It was never enough, until I couldn't take it any more.

I hear that Europe and America are gradually getting further apart, as lava bubbles up into the gap between the tectonic plates in Iceland. I see geology not just on a large but on a small scale in how sand grades itself. Different beaches in Orkney have different-sized pebbles; some areas are formed of whole shells, some broken fragments, others just tiny grains of sand. There's a cove at the north-east of the island where the sand is mostly made up of iron from a shipwreck. I find fossils of raindrops from two billion years ago, souvenirs from a time when the sun was further away from the earth.

In grandiose moments, high on fresh air and freedom on the hill, I study my personal geology. My body is a continent. Forces are at work in the night. A bruxist, I grind my teeth in my sleep, like tectonic plates. When I blink the sun flickers, my breath pushes the clouds across the sky and the waves roll into the shore in time with my beating heart. Lightning strikes every time I sneeze, and when I orgasm, there's an earthquake. The islands' headlands rise above the sea, like my limbs in the bathtub, my freckles are famous landmarks and my tears rivers. My lovers are tectonic plates and stone cathedrals.

23

TRIDUANA

I DON'T GO TO THE SOUTH of the island often – without a
car in the winter, getting to the shop is usually far enough
– but today I visit the Loch of Tredwell for the first time. I
leave my bike when the going gets too boggy and proceed on
foot through the tufty 'links', the sandy land that connects the
sea, the bay and the loch. This is a different habitat again from
the exposed heath of the North Hill – marshy, with semi-
submerged gates and fence posts, a watery half-land.

I disturb grazing geese and they fly off, shifting smoothly from
parallel lines into a V formation. Over a weekend in the autumn,
more than 21,000 breeding greylag geese were counted in Orkney:
there are now officially more geese than humans on the isles.
During winter, with migrant birds from the north, numbers increase
to around 76,000, roughly half of Iceland's greylag population.
The success of the birds makes them a pest to farmers, whose
grass they eat, and over recent months hundreds have been shot.

A dome-shaped promontory jutting into the loch is, as Jocelyn Rendall of Holland Farm describes in her guide to Papay, 'crowned with a tantalising confusion of ruined buildings'. This small circular peninsula, once an island, is an early Christian site, with the remains of a chapel dating back to around the eighth century. As with many important places, the chapel was built on the site of much older constructions, with archaeological remains – a wall and bank – that have been dated to the Iron Age. When the site was first excavated by Papay's laird in 1879, underground passages were found along the lochside.

I sit at the top of the mound and smoke. I can see why this has been a special place over the centuries. Like the Ring of Brodgar on the Mainland, it feels at the heart of the island, encircled by a ring of loch, then land, then sea, with fine views across to the Holm and other islands beyond. In Orkney, land is often just a thin division between sky and water: the sea or a loch is nearly always in view.

Aerial photographs of the promontory show its concentric circles and the chapel within. This afternoon, the darkening sky is reflected on the different bodies of water – the loch rippled by the wind, the sea churning with the tide. The small plane flies over on its way back to the Mainland with propellers humming. I am calmed by the peace and beauty of the place.

St Tredwell, also known as Triduana, a 'holy virgin' or nun, was courted by Pictish King Nechtan, who admired her beautiful eyes. In response, Triduana gouged them out and sent them to him, skewered on a thorn. I read different accounts of the story, some saying that the king tried to rape her and her actions were self-preservation, others suggesting it was an act of love.

The story of Tredwell is slippery. She may have been a pagan goddess who was reinvented in a saintly guise. Papay is 'associated' with her and has a claim to be her burial place; some even say that she lived alone in the chapel in the loch. It is more likely that her bones, or relics associated with her, were carried here a long time after her death, if indeed she existed at all.

There is a string of wells and other sites dedicated to Triduana in the north of Scotland. A stained-glass window depicting her, serene and haloed, is in St Magnus Cathedral, the light she could no longer see shining through.

By the twelfth century, the chapel in the loch became a place of pilgrimage, particularly for the blind or those with eye trouble. Pilgrims thought that on Papay they would find the cure they were seeking and travelled here from all over Orkney and beyond. An account in the Orkneyinga Saga tells of Earl Harald Maddadsson, tortured in 1201, 'his tongue cut out and a knife driven into his eyes', then taken to 'where St Tredwell rests, and there he was restored to health in both speech and sight'.

The faithful were still travelling here five hundred years later in 1700, when Presbyterian minister John Brand describes the 'Superstitious People' making pilgrimage to the site. 'Such as are able to walk used to go so many times about the loch as they think will perfect the cure before they make any use of the water, and that is without speaking any, for they believe that if they speak this will mar the cure.' It is said pilgrims walked three times around the loch, then bathed their eyes in its healing waters.

My aversion to religion – and my mum's Church in particular – made me reluctant to begin the 12 Steps. I avoid thinking or talking about God and faith – it makes my heart beat faster and anger rise inside me. In AA, they say this type of 'resentment' is often what leads to drinking. Although I don't want to get rid of my cool, rational mind, I do want to stay sober so I know I must, like they told me in the treatment centre, face these feelings.

I did believe once. From a young age, my brother and I went to church with Mum. It was not the conventional Church of Scotland, which is dotted around the islands, with dwindling congregations except at weddings and funerals. It was an all-pervading choice, a way of life.

The Orkney Christian Fellowship held meetings in schools and community centres. There were not hymns but worshipful pop songs, with guitars and arms raised, whoops of hallelujah. I watched charismatic preachers and theatrical salvations, heard the language of 'born again', 'the Holy Spirit', 'being saved' and 'bearing witness'.

I was taught that the Church was the people not the building. I was taught that we needed to ask Jesus into our hearts. I was taught that hell and the devil were real. When I was twelve, I went to a 'Lessons in Love' weekend and was told that homosexuality and masturbation were wrong. I talked in tongues. When I was thirteen, and suffering from headaches that doctors couldn't provide a reason for, Mum took me south to a conference held by an American evangelist preacher where I saw queues of sick and afflicted believers touched by him on the forehead then falling to the floor, 'slain in the spirit'.

The new recruits to Mum's Church were often people who, like her, had moved to Orkney and were struggling. The leaders were well meaning but also domineering, imposing their views and style of worship on others.

When I was about fourteen, I started listening to things that other people, including my father, were saying. I had influences outside the Church. In my teenage years I swung from religion to rock and roll, from reading modern American translations of the Bible to dead poets and music magazines. My childhood moved between the freedom of the farm and Church-influenced discipline.

I stopped going to church. I no longer believed. I screamed at Mum that I would never be the daughter she wanted: I was never going to follow Jesus and I was going to hell. Later, I'd often – arrogantly, spitefully – compare Mum's experience in church on a Sunday morning, arms aloft, singing, transported, to mine in a club on a Saturday night. 'But,' I'd say with a flourish, 'at least I know I'm deluded.'

Once you've been baptised it is hard to go back. This kind of belief is so strong it alienates the believer from other people – from friends, from family.

★   ★   ★

Step Three suggests that we 'made a decision to turn our will and our lives over to the care of God as we understood Him'. I am resistant to giving up control and think it is impossible for anyone to do this: we still have to make decisions. But Dee asks me to think about 'turning something over' as simply looking at things from a different angle. It is possible to think of AA's 'God stuff' as another way of thinking in order to recover. Addicts have to learn to restrain their egos – the intellects that have run us aground. My thinking processes seem to have got me into trouble so far so surely it is worthwhile to try to behave differently.

The programme is, in fact, not that mystical. It often resembles cognitive behavioural therapy, with advice about recognising damaging thought patterns and behaviours and attempting to change them, and suggestions to take a step back and consider the consequences before acting.

I am struggling with my thoughts. It is as if there are two separate parts of myself: the one that took me to rehab and AA meetings and who hasn't drunk for twenty-two months and twenty days; and the one on the other side, dreaming of a bottle of wine and feeling as if this, despite my actions, is somehow the 'real me'. I don't want to let go. There are battles inside me.

I have good eyesight and little faith but today, as a gesture towards trying new things, I recreate the pilgrims' ritual, walking around the loch anticlockwise. According to the GPS tracker on my phone, the circumnavigation is 3.1 miles and takes me seventy-eight minutes. I duck under electric fences, climb over barbed wire and balance along the tops of stone dykes. The ground is marshy with uneven turf and water sloshes up around my wellies. Halfway around the rain starts, blowing into my face off the sea. I think about someone sick carrying out this walk, someone half blind in skirts and petticoats, making the loop three times in silence.

By coming here to Papay, I am following the route taken by desperate pilgrims, who'd made difficult journeys to reach this holy isle. It was a special place even back in the days of the Vikings, and the Orkneyinga Saga describes how the body of Earl Rognvald was carried to Papa Westray for burial.

Did Triduana walk the shores of this loch? I wonder how she might have felt, a beautiful young woman, her energies and beliefs so strong that she could hurt herself so violently. Her act of romance or chaste fervour showed a strength of conviction that created a centuries-long cult.

Breaking the peace of my lochside trudge, a swooping hen harrier terrifies and flushes assorted ducks and waders from the loch. I rub the scar on the back of my head. I picture myself midway through a backwards roll, attached to bungee cords, on a trampoline. I am caught between places: here on Papay but my mind in the internet and London, resisting a 'spiritual programme' but wanting to get better.

Incomers to islands, these days, are still often either looking for or running away from something. What am I expecting from this ritual? Do I somehow think that coming here, bravely facing the winter alone, will make me a better person or cure me? Am I hoping for a miracle? If I walk the right configuration round the loch, will Triduana remove my addiction?

When I am in motion I am at ease, able to move forward mentally as well as physically. I use walking and swimming to calm my churning thoughts. My sea swims are increasingly important in relieving the non-specific low-level anxiety I often feel. The cold water shocks out any mental stress – my body suddenly has something more immediate to deal with. In this way, swimming is a mild form of the ECT Dad was given.

When I complete the circuit, I walk the periphery of the promontory before carefully following the walls of the two inner circles, making sure that the shapes would be picked up by my GPS tracker. In my notebook, I have written my own 'Step Three prayer', suggested as part of the 12 Steps process. Examples that I have read mention God or mystical powers that I can't honestly believe in so my statement goes only as far as I am comfortable. I pick up a small stone from the promontory. I begin to read my prayer out loud. The idea of praying is almost repulsive to me but as I speak I gain confidence and volume. Thinking about the idea of 'turning it over', I throw the stone into the loch, watching the ripples it leaves until they disappear.

I've been deep-sea dream-walking, tipping eyelashes out of my computer keyboard, grinding my teeth, but right now I'm relaxed. This chapel in the loch is a place of retreat, a well-defended lookout. I think of the eyes of Triduana on a stick. I think of the eyes of the last great auk, preserved in spirits and stored in Copenhagen's Zoological Museum, staring out for ever.

I don't hate Mum and her Church for what they taught me, any more than I hate the ancient pilgrims for seeking their cure. In some ways, I admire the evangelicals' conviction. What is the point of religion if you don't really believe? If their interpretation of the Bible is correct and all the unsaved are going to hell, surely believers should be out there, screaming it.

Religion is another way of attempting to access the transcendental, seeking the same highs of experience and places of comfort that others find at raves, in drunkenness, in love, in superstition, in mania. Without these things, life lies flat. Now, despite its extreme form, I wouldn't take Mum's faith away from her.

The loch is still again, my stone sunk among the relics and collapsed tunnels. I am not a devout eighth-century Celtic girl with a bandage around her eyes, I'm a twenty-first-century heathen with my scarf wrapped around my head, wearing wellies on a BMX. I must get a move on: my hands are cold and the shop is open only for two hours on a Friday.

24

FAIR ISLE

O N Papay, fair isle has been a spectre at the edge of my field of vision, just over the horizon. A reproduction of a 1654 map of Orkney and Shetland hangs over the kitchen table showing 'The Faire Yle', a detail-free outline halfway between the two island groups. Orkney and Shetland are in the Fair Isle sea area of the shipping forecast and, getting ready for bed, my ears tune in when its name is read: 'Wind: easterly or north-easterly six to gale eight. Sea state: rough or very rough. Wintry showers. Visibility: good, occasionally poor.'

There's so much sky here in Orkney and I watch the ever-changing weather approaching. In northerly winds on Papay, it comes over the North Hill from Fair Isle. Short-term weather forecasting is best done by looking out of the window but I also check internet forecasts avidly. As well as the BBC weather site, I look at Northern Isles Weather, a website run by Dave Wheeler on Fair Isle. I like imagining him as a renegade meteorologist, operating independently on that far-flung isle, just north of view.

On Hogmanay I'm told that some people in Papay are descended from a family of Irvines who came here from Fair Isle, and Irvine's Geo at the north of the island is where their boat came ashore. Living conditions on Fair Isle in the early nineteenth century were so tough that even life on Papay looked appealing. The family loaded their possessions into a small boat and rowed south, probably not knowing exactly where they would wash up. They would never see their home again, apart from on the horizon on a clear day.

As mentions of the isle keep coming up, my notion of visiting grows and becomes irresistible. On 'Mad Friday', as they call the last Friday before Christmas in the pubs in Kirkwall, when, it seems to me, everyone else is out getting lashed at parties, I make a reckless plan to visit in early January: I'll take the overnight ferry from Kirkwall to Lerwick in Shetland (Fair Isle is officially part of Shetland), then fly out to Fair Isle. When I book the flights, I'm warned that I might be stuck there for longer than planned. At this time of year, the ferry and planes are often delayed by weather: fog, wind or rough seas.

On the thirteenth day of Christmas, I am the only passenger, alongside a backlog of post bags, on the Islander plane to Fair Isle from Tingwall airport on mainland Shetland. From above, I see Shetland sheep grazing on cliffs' edges in precarious pairs. To the west looms the chunk of the island of Foula. We fly over miles of water before Fair Isle appears on the horizon, rising spectacularly from the sea. On a map it looks a similar area to

Papay, and official statistics give areas of 7.68 km² for Fair Isle and 9.18 km² for Papay but, now I'm here, the elevation of the island – rising to Ward Hill at 217 metres and edged with sheer cliffs and high slopes of grass and rubble – makes it seem bigger.

It is an unusually mild day for the time of year and I walk to the north of the island, to the North Lighthouse, where a narrow walkway stretches out across a dizzying drop to a disused foghorn. Fair Isle has the same size population as Papay, around seventy, all living in the south of the island, mainly in white croft houses owned by the National Trust for Scotland. The houses are nestled in against the harsh climate and ever-close sea. Whereas on Papay we can see other islands surrounding us, here there is simply ocean and it feels more remote and exposed to the weather. Fair Isle is not only the UK's most remote inhabited island (although Foula also has claim to this) but the UK's windiest place, alongside Tiree in the Hebrides.

Fair Isle is unlike anywhere I've been, apart perhaps from the valley of Rackwick on Hoy, where an isolated village lies on a bay between cliff-edged hills. Everywhere you turn there are dramatic views of the coastline, sweeping curves cut off by towering cliffs. The improbable ski slope of Sheep Rock gives the island a distinctive profile, and it seems preposterous that, until 1977, sheep were kept there, winched on and off one by one, using ropes, from and to boats far below.

A bird hide has been built straight up from a cliff and I edge inside. The cliffs are busy with fulmars so in the breeding season it must be teeming. A black-backed gull is perched on the peak of an iceberg-shaped skerry, like a pirate king.

Fair Isle is famous for its bird observatory, bringing orni-
thologists to see its breeding seabird colonies as well as to find
migrating rarities in spring and autumn. As the only piece of
land in a large area of sea, on the flight path between Scandinavia,
Iceland, the Faroes and the rest of Europe, birds are drawn in,
more common species and prized rarities. Valleys on the island
are sprung with Heligoland traps – funnels to catch and study
birds.

I lose my balance climbing over a stile and plunge onto the
grass. When I pull myself up, a bit shaken, and look back over
the dyke, I see a car stop. The driver gets out, slings a dead sheep
out of the boot then kicks it over the edge of the geo, down
the cliff, into the sea below. There is a lot of edge here.

I had slept only intermittently on the overnight ferry up from
Orkney the night before and the spring-like weather makes me
think I could have a snooze in a sheltered hollow, wrapped in
my waterproofs, but the cold from my stone pillow reminds me
it is January. I had been kept awake by the swelling North Sea
churning the boat and my stomach, and by the Orkneyinga Saga.
I was reading of tenth-century Norse earls sailing over the same
waters that were rocking me, locating myself in space and history.

Fair Isle was of vital strategic importance in the times of the
sagas. A beacon was built on the isle that could be lit to warn
Earl Paul in Orkney if Earl Rognvald from Shetland was
approaching by ship. However, Rognvald was one step ahead
and sent out a dummy ship: 'When the beacon on Fair Isle was
seen to be alight, Thorstein Rognuson had the beacon lit on
North Ronaldsay, and so one after another was lit throughout

the islands. All the farmers gathered around the Earl, making up a sizeable army.'

After this false alarm, Rognvald sent a spy to Fair Isle. 'Uni chose three young Shetlanders to come with him in a six-oared boat with provisions and fishing tackle and rowed over to Fair Isle.' Pretending that he was a Norwegian wronged by Earl Rognvald, Uni volunteered for the job of looking after the Fair Isle beacon. When Rognvald's real ships approached, Uni was found to have disappeared and the beacon was soaked with water so it wouldn't light. The warning would not reach Orkney that night and no army was raised.

As the captain ding-dongs over the intercom at six a.m. to tell the passengers we are approaching Lerwick, I imagine fires being lit one by one on the hilltops, like our modern lighthouses, points of light in the dark seas.

As well as being Fair Isle's weatherman, Dave Wheeler is the airport manager, a crofter and the registrar, keeping the official records of the island's births, deaths and marriages. He is also a professional photographer and teaches an IT class at the school (roll: six, the same as Papay). When Dave, a Yorkshireman, arrived in the early seventies, he was able to convince the Met Office that they needed a Fair Isle recording station, plugging a gap in the weather recording network. 'You have to find a niche,' he explains of island life, and describes how he and his wife Jane brought over cows, a rarity on the island, and sell their milk. I think of my own parents, coming to Orkney in the seventies, the photos of them in woolly jumpers with different hairstyles.

Although some of his weather-recording equipment has now been automated, each day Dave sends regular reports to the Met Office, starting at six a.m. and carrying on into the night. He shows me the meteorological enclosure on his croft, 'Field', in the shadow of Sheep Rock. Thermometers measure air, grass and underground temperature; an anemometer on a post at ten metres height, the Met standard, measures winds; a beautiful device that looks like a crystal ball records sunshine. The glass sphere is a burning lens, Dave explains, focusing the sun's rays onto a strip of card marked off in hours, so length of burn – sunshine – can be measured. The card is changed daily after sunset.

I look through a collection of shots taken by Dave's fixed webcam over just a few months with the same field of vision and shutter speed. It takes a picture every hour and the huge changes in weather and light, in seasons and over days, are shown in the changes in the pictures. I see the colours transform from green grass and blue skies to washed-out fields at the end of winter. In the mornings, sunlit from behind, Sheep Rock appears in shadow but in the evening the details of the cliff are sharply revealed. A sunset casts everything – sky, cliffs, hillside – in pink. There are grey skies and whiteouts. Sometimes Sheep Rock is obscured by fog and at others the lens of the camera is splashed with rain. On very bright days, the sun appears as a black dot, the camera unable to process its light.

* * *

The wind means I will not get off the island the next day as I planned. As others predicted, the planes are cancelled. I start to think about the difference between choosing to come to an island and being stuck there, stranded. As a teenager I'd shouted, 'I didn't ask to be born here,' and hated having to get lifts from my parents to go anywhere, weather howling every time I stepped outside the door.

I spend an extra night in the old lighthouse keeper's accommodation at the South Lighthouse, built in 1890 and automated in 1998. The foghorn at the front, which could be heard forty kilometres away, was turned off in 2005. The lawns around the lighthouse look as if they are maintained by a groundskeeper but in fact they are kept short by the whipping wind and sea salt.

I walk the coastline listening to BBC foreign correspondents, feeling like a dot in the ocean. I decide I want to walk to the top of Malcolm's Head, which some say was the site of the saga's beacons – a foolhardy plan in this gale. I ascend the hill in a crouched position, probably watched by amused islanders in the houses below. I lie forward into the wind, like a mattress of air: it takes my breath and exhausts me – a full-body experience. It's loud enough to hide in. Chunks of sea foam are being blown over the cliff into my face. I think it's calmed, then a powerful gust blows up again.

As well as birders, visitors to the lighthouse include 'island-baggers', who want to visit as many Scottish islands as possible. The 1861 census defined an island as 'any piece of solid land surrounded by water which affords sufficient vegetation to support one or two sheep, or is inhabited by man'. Haswell-Smith's guide snootily denies island status to Skye, joined by a bridge, and Orkney's Burray and South Ronaldsay, joined to the Mainland in the Second World War by the Churchill Barriers, built to stop German U-boats. There are also 'lighthouse-baggers', and 'Marilyn-baggers', who have perhaps finished the challenge of climbing all the Munros, hills in Scotland of more than 3,000 feet (915 metres) and are moving on to the Marilyns, more than 490 feet (150 metres), of which Fair Isle's Ward Hill is one.

Another reason that people come to Fair Isle is to trace family history. There are thousands of descendants of Fair Isle people, with surnames like Stout and Irvine, all over Canada and the USA. When I mention my trip, several Orcadian friends tell me their great-grandparents originally came from the isle. My friend Rognvald Leslie shows me a photograph of his great-grandfather, George Leslie, striking both for his dapper handsomeness and his slightly exotic features, which almost look Mongolian, Inuit or Sami. This may be coincidental but Fair Islers may like to feel kinship with edge-landers, tough people from the far north. Rognvald says that George lived at a croft called Pund, which Dave tells me is one of the only two derelict houses on the island – when most places are abandoned the stones are quickly claimed for another building – and points me in its direction. In the mist, I pick around the broken-down remains of the house, now used for storing animal feed, and outbuildings. I discover that Pund is where the Duchess of Bedford stayed when she came on bird-watching trips in the early twentieth century and am excited to tell Rognvald of his aristocratic links.

I am a rare January visitor so people on the island know I am there before I meet them. The woman in the shop knows where I'm staying. But what am I doing here on Fair Isle in January, a single woman with no easy explanation? I'm not a birder or someone tracing my family history. I'm not sure. It's just that I've been scrolling over Google Maps and reading Wikis for ages and now I'm here. My leisure time is no longer filled with drinking and nights out, and I don't have children or many responsibilities, so this is what I'm doing instead, visiting increasingly remote northern places, following the map to the edge. This is the story of what happens after you stop drinking. This is the freedom of sobriety.

I didn't know what would happen when I got sober, when I launched myself into the unknown future. I didn't know I would return to Orkney. I didn't know my strongest desire would be to hear the rasping call of the corncrake. I didn't know I'd start swimming in the sea and taking my writing more seriously. I didn't know I'd find myself alone climbing a steep hill on the country's most remote island during a gale in early January, buffeted by spindrift. But I had to give myself the chance to find out.

There are disputes over the origin of the name 'Fair Isle'. It could be from the same root as 'fairway' or 'thoroughfare', a place to navigate by, halfway between Orkney and Shetland. I find it weirdly prescient that Fair Isle is located such that the

nearest places – North Ronaldsay in Orkney and Sumburgh
Head in Shetland – are both just on the horizon, around twenty-
six miles away. It is almost completely isolated, but not quite.
North Ronaldsay lighthouse is the tallest land lighthouse in
Britain so its light can be seen from Fair Isle. Another idea is
that it is simply called 'Fair' because it's bonny.

A notorious site of numerous shipwrecks, Fair Isle has had
different methods for warning of its rocky dangers. As well as
the two lighthouses and foghorns, there is a rocket station, built
in 1885 and used only for a year, as an alternative to the foghorn,
to warn passing ships about the presence of the isle. During
thick fog or snow it fired rockets at ten-minute intervals,
exploding 800 feet above sea level. Next to the site of the Viking
beacons, at the top of Malcolm's Head, is a nineteenth-century
watchtower, erected during the Napoleonic Wars to look out
for enemy ships. On Ward Hill are the remains of a Second
World War radar station and coastguards' huts used to scan the
ocean by eye for seafarers in distress.

Fair Isle is no longer important for military defence but its
location, as an outlier miles from anywhere, is important strat-
egically for meteorological and ornithological records.

On my last night on Fair Isle, about an hour after I fall
asleep, an asteroid passes relatively close to earth. Asteroid 99942
Apophis once caused fears when it was calculated to have a
2.9 per cent chance of hitting the earth in 2029 but, with each
year, astronomers refine their model of its trajectory and tonight
it passes more than eight million miles away. There are ten
asteroids out there with a higher risk rating than Apophis,

monitored from an office in California using information from powerful telescopes.

From my bedroom window in the lighthouse, in the haar, four beams pass every thirty seconds as the light rotates, its characteristic pattern. (Out to sea these beams are seen as flashes and I recognise them a couple of nights later, out on deck around nine o'clock on the ferry returning to Orkney.) Back inside the lighthouse, I fall asleep under the beams and dream of warning systems: beacons, rockets, lighthouses, satellites and telescopes. I dream of the dangers and curiosities we try to predict, measure and bag, coming towards us on this small isle, over the sea, through the sky and across outer space.

25

BONFIRE

O N THE WALL OF THE treatment centre, among the peers' work from the art-therapy classes – rainbows, inspirational slogans – there was a felt-tip drawing of a dog with its tail on fire. I used to look at it during the interminable group-therapy sessions. It spoke to me somehow.

In my last week on the programme, a new lad joined. It was, as is often the case, his second time through and I found out, to my joy, that he was the artist. Pleased that someone liked his work, he was happy to give me the drawing as a leaving gift and I have it with me now, a dog with its tail on fire, hanging on the wall of Rose Cottage, as a reminder of those twelve weeks and that this was my last chance: I don't want to go through the system again and be trapped in the cycle. It's also a reminder that if I smell something burning it's probably myself.

★　　★　　★

There is some excitement on Papay at the arrival of a skip. Large rubbish is stored up for these occasions, to be taken off the island, rather than the old method of tipping it over a cliff. Historically, dead sheep were disposed of by being thrown over the cliff – on our farm, into Nebo Geo. Now this is illegal and Dad has a metal tank out at the far side of a field where the bodies are left to decompose. I catch a whiff of rotting flesh when I walk by.

Bonfires are another method of rubbish-disposal, popular here, and most houses have a blackened patch in the yard. Plumes of flame and smoke rise from the low island on still days and often on Sundays. Despite our small population, there are three different church groups here – Church of Scotland, a Gospel Hall and a Quaker meeting – but these fires are a link to something pre-Christian.

Papay has its own fire brigade, made up of five or so locals who are paid a retainer although the time commitment and training mean it's hard to make up a full crew. Living in the city, I'd got used to local-authority-run fireworks displays, with safety barriers and officials in hi-vis vests. But I remember the bonfires once a week on the farm and the smell of burning black plastic from silage bales. We're in control of our own fires here.

As well as for practical purposes, there are bonfires on Papay for celebrations and special occasions. For the last three years, in mid-February, a contemporary art festival has taken place on the island: Papay Gyro Nights, set up by Papay residents and artists Ivanov and Tsz Chan, a couple who moved to the island about five years ago and have a Papay-born daughter. That an art festival is held here at all is surprising, even more so that it's in the off-season when gales thrash and nights are dark and long.

The ancient Papay tradition of the Night of the Gyros was celebrated until the early twentieth century on the first full moon of February. Young boys went out into the winter night, chased by older boys to 'weep them with a tangle under the full moon's light'. The last known celebration was in 1914 but now, a hundred years later, the art festival is reviving the tradition with a modern interpretation.

The bias of the festival is towards experimental video art. Some artists have made the journey to Papay, alongside a small but enthusiastic group of international visitors and curious Orcadians. The hostel is pretty much full for the week – unheard of at this time of year – and island women make meals for everyone.

It is amusing to see islanders and visitors, from kids to old folks, farmers and performance artists, standing in the cold kelp store dutifully watching an hour-long experimental film, where masked figures perform strange rituals. It's a much more diverse and attentive audience than there would be in a London gallery, although I notice some people slip out with the excuse of sleepy children. There is a general open-mindedness on Papay, a feeling that, although the art might not be for everyone, it is making something happen and bringing people to the island.

A Norwegian artist spends the week producing a 'kinetic sculpture' in and around an abandoned croft near Rose Cottage. I watch him through my telescope, battling to hang a canvas in the wind. An anthropologist from Minnesota gives a lecture, the projector set up on a giant sperm whale vertebra. A Frog King from Hong Kong makes his nest in the school.

I remember how, on the first Thursday of each month, art galleries around east London were open late, with people walking between them as much for the free drink as the art. Girls in exaggerated head bows and boys in old men's jackets drank cans of lager in the street. Hopeful artists inhabited these nights, displaying photographs of urban romance, keeping quiet about how they spent their days and paid their rent.

One night I accidentally destroyed the art. Elaborate foil 'pieces' were suspended from steel wires and dangled into the lobby of the gallery, like chandeliers, and, being a curious and sloshed viewer, I leaned over the balcony and hoisted one up. A security guard came and tapped me on the shoulder so I immediately dropped the wire, snapping it and sending the art smashing to the ground. It made a terrific noise.

Gyro Nights launches an architectural competition to design a bonfire – a 'combustible centrepiece' – to be constructed and burned at the festival, and they receive entries from around the world. Architecture students look at Papay on Google Maps to find the best location for their fire: a structure whose purpose is its own destruction. A bonfire is a type of controlled chaos. On the first night of the festival, we take part in a torch-lit procession, from the shop down the hill to the old pier where we put our flaming wooden torches together to light a fire.

Coming to this island without light pollution, I remember just how dark it can get. At midwinter I close my curtains at half past three. In days gone by, four times every year, hilltops across Orkney blazed with orange firelight. Giant bonfires were constructed and lit to commemorate the ancient festivals of Yule, Beltane, Johnsmas and Hallowmas. In the seventeenth century, cattle, horses, the sick or infirm were led 'sunwise' around bonfires because the flames were believed to have a purifying or revitalising power. In the past they would burn heather and peat; today it's more likely to be packaging pallets or old fence posts. The fires light up the winter nights, giving excitement and hope.

The full moon and new moons of winter – including the full moon of Gyro Nights – are also the times when it's possible to forage for spoots, the local name for razor fish or razor shells, long, thin shellfish that can be caught without the need for a boat, at the lowest tides.

At new moon, Tim shows me the best spot on the beach where the 'spoot sand' is exposed at the ebb tide. We walk backwards and the spoots, which lie vertically just under the surface, are disturbed by our booming footsteps and burrow downwards, leaving a telltale bubble in the sand. By walking backwards, I am able to spot these bubbles – the 'spoot' of water – and dig furiously with a trowel, then with my rubber-gloved hands. I feel the razor fish pulling downwards away from me and it's a battle of woman versus spoot but I manage to get it and put it into my bucket. That night I fry them up with some garlic and eat them with spaghetti – a small meal but one of the most satisfying I've had in a long time, caught for free and with fun.

I have been sober for exactly twenty-three months. I remember 21 February as being Said's 'clean date' because we had to repeat these to each other once a week in the treatment centre. He was one of the very few others that got through the three months of treatment without 'picking up' but I haven't spoken to him for more than a year. My last text, a few months ago, went unanswered. I try another. It doesn't feel good.

I text another person I became friendly with in the centre, a funny, fragile girl with jewelled fingernails and more problems than just the drink, including a history of anorexia and relationships with abusive men. She was thrown out of the programme halfway through after admitting taking some of her boyfriend's prescription painkillers one night when she was feeling desperate. The rule was zero tolerance. I saw her later in AA meetings and she was back drinking, getting a few weeks sober then relapse after relapse. She replies telling me she is in a psychiatric unit after getting arrested for breach of the peace.

I've also been thinking about another woman I met on the programme. She had come from a residential rehab, where she had been living with her baby son, and had been off heroin for nine months but was honest about the way she felt: 'I'm not comfortable in my skin', 'I still want to take drugs.' She didn't just say what they wanted to hear, talking shamelessly about her 'sugar daddy', saying the groups were boring, fidgeting and struggling to complete the work.

She was moving from a B&B into a local-authority halfway house, and I offered to help carry her bags but, unsurprisingly, she didn't turn up at the agreed time and place and couldn't be reached on the phone. After that weekend she didn't come back to the centre and I'm almost certain that she's back to her old life, working as a prostitute, using heroin, and that her son has been taken away from her.

I think for some people it's gone too far, that all the help in the world isn't going to make them go straight, and the trappings of a normal life will always be frustrating. I've been thinking about her because, although I'm much more adjusted to sobriety, I know how she felt: trapped, dissatisfied. But I also know she will not be happy now, out there.

As I remember these people – my friends – and think about how their lives will be back in active addiction, I know with increasing certainty that I can't and won't go back.

It is a clear, still evening, and the smell of paraffin lingers in the air under bright stars. As we are led down the hill to the bonfire by the Frog King, I momentarily think this would be more fun if I was drinking. Being sober at celebratory occasions still feels weird. Alcohol gave me the ability to be in the present. It lifted anxiety and gave me that initial buzz. I was more lively and confident after a few.

But I shake my head when someone offers me a hip flask. I'm smiling. The person with the whisky has no idea. This is no longer an option for me. For those of us for whom things went so far we ended up in rehab, addicted, the reality is that not stopping drinking or taking drugs will lead, maybe terrifyingly soon, to insanity, incarceration or death. I must find new kinds of fun and new ways to celebrate.

I see the Norwegian artist through the smoke and he smiles at me. The day before I'd met him on the beach. He was carrying a plastic bag containing six types of seaweed. He is about the same age and height as me and also has long blond hair. He feels a bit like a male version of myself – a nomadic artist who's washed up on this island for a short time.

I often feel the same as I used to. I want to make connections and to communicate because we are only and really alive right now. I still want to experience the extremes so I must find ways to fulfil this need sober. I must be brave. I wonder if I can still be cheeky or flirtatious without booze. If I master this, I could be unstoppable. In the past months I've been stifled by bruised confidence and anxiety, but these things take time. I'm gradually learning to say things sober that other people wait to say drunk.

When I was drinking I wanted to have exciting experiences but I was lazy and unimaginative, expecting the mere act of getting messed up to be enough to make something happen. For every time I made a new friend and ended up back at their house trying on their dresses, while discussing our favourite writers, there would be more occasions when I'd find myself alone and stumbling at three a.m., without my jacket, trying to find a night bus home.

I'm offered a lift home from the bonfire but decline: I'm talking to the sculptor. He touches my arm. The Pleiades are visible and I suggest we walk along the coast under the stars. Passing North Wick, I tell him about the selkies, how they are the souls of people who have drowned, condemned for ever to swim in the sea.

Back at Rose Cottage, I light the fire and we sit either side of it, talking about seaweed, families and art. I slip off my shoes and put my feet on the edge of his chair and, still talking and looking at me, he puts his hand on my ankle. My body soaks up this point of contact with relief and pleasure. Being touched soothes months of loneliness. I know suddenly, from this one touch, that sex is possible not only tonight but also in my future, although he's leaving the island in the morning and returning to Scandinavia. Life is opening up and stretches ahead, sparkling with possibility. He's stroking my other ankle and the conversation is faltering.

I want to develop hardihood – boldness and daring. I am looking to the ways they did things in the past, ancient festivals and celebrations for the changes of the seasons. I'm looking for new enchantments to lift the spirits in late winter when the wind seems to change direction to face me whichever way I walk. I'm trying to drink up these times on the island because I know I'll miss them when they're gone. I've already wasted too much time.

I hear of how, in 1952, a whole hill on the Mainland caught

alight. The flames rolled with the wind, lighting the night. At this time of year, hybrid beings emerge and mingle with people, ancestral beings return from the dead, we forage for molluscs and light the dark sky with fire. These are times for people to come together and liven each other's spirits, burning the past.

26

UNDERSEA

THERE ARE THINGS I REMEMBER. A farm tom cat went missing, out chasing rabbits on the Outrun, and returned months later, twice his old size, face scarred with half his whiskers missing, walking confidently into his old home and scaring us. I remember Dad walking home from Stromness in bare feet, seven miles as the crow flies across fields and fences, leaving possessions along the way and coming through the door early in the morning when we were still in bed, ranting about a black bull.

When doctors ask, I say there is no history of heart disease, cancer or diabetes in my family. Mental illness is another matter. It's on both sides. Mum's dad was also a manic depressive and only recently I learned that a paternal great-grandmother committed suicide. There were times I thought that if I stopped drinking I would discover that I was bipolar too, that I was just self-medicating. If I were to go mad, it would come as no surprise at all.

Some aspects of my childhood didn't seem unusual until I moved away from Orkney and looked back. As teenagers, we picked winkles from the shore and sold them by the bucket, by weight, to a local shellfish dealer, who sent them to Spain or to be used for water purification in fish farms. I remember summer days up at the peat hill at the centre of the Mainland where farms are assigned a patch to cut peat, to be burned over winter. While Mum and Dad worked, stamping down the cutters and slicing up the millennia-old bog into bricks, I'd crawl, eyes at ground-level among cotton grass and water-skating insects.

Tom and I found scores of jellyfish washed up in a geo at the farm. There were so many that they coated the rocks and we picked our way among them, distressed. One by one, we picked up the cool gelatinous animals in our arms, some of them breaking, carried them to the shoreline and placed them back in the sea. This species – moon jellyfish – doesn't sting but leaves a mild envenomation and our bare arms and hands were red and buzzing but we didn't care: we were children performing a disaster-relief mission, running over slidy pebbles with armfuls of wobbling transparent pink.

These mass 'strandings' of jellyfish happen when currents wash a swarm into shore, often in spring. Jellyfish are only capable of upwards independent movement so are moved horizontally by currents and tides. The names of jellyfish and hydromedusae found around UK coasts are poetry: blue, compass, by-the-wind-sailor, moon, lion's mane, mauve, Portuguese man o' war. Moon jellyfish, *Aurelia aurita*, are transparent with a hint of pink, and blue rings inside – their reproductive organs. Jellyfish are the outline of a creature barely there, drifting in the currents, pelagic and intangible.

I have been looking, amazed, at some underwater photographs. Strange and beautiful creatures and bright colours suggest the tropics but the pictures were all taken in Orkney waters, in the shallows close to shore. Local snorkellers find and photograph many species of fish, shellfish, anemones and jellyfish. They see sea urchins, sponges, starfish and sea slugs.

My friend Anne from the RSPB comes out to Papay from the Mainland to show me how to snorkel. At a rocky area of North Wick Bay, we put on wetsuits, neoprene boots, gloves and hoods, flippers and snorkel masks, and slip into the water, like less-elegant seals.

My first time snorkelling hits me with several new sensations: first, being in the water with the protection of the wetsuit and breathing through the snorkel, but second, and most memorable, looking under water, close to the seabed, able to see clearly what's usually hidden. Although today the tide is too high and wind too strong for ideal snorkelling conditions, the dip is enough to get an idea of the 'different world' Anne talks enthusiastically about entering.

Anne leaves me with a set of snorkel gear, and at low tide after the next full moon, I go out to try it alone. Walking down to the sea, I feel nervous about getting cold or swept out, and I choose a sheltered spot at the corner of the bay known as

Weelie's Taing, circled by rocks like a lagoon. I crawl into the shallow water on my face and after a few minutes I realise that I am breathing easily through the snorkel and don't feel cold in the wetsuit. I begin to relax and enjoy it.

I don't have to keep moving, I just float on my front, observing what's around, moving with the tide, like a corpse. I forget I am floating on the surface and feel I am deep on the ocean bed. I use my hands to drag myself over the rocks, parting seaweed, looking for sunken treasure. Hermit crabs cram themselves back into their shells at my approach. I see red anemones and paddle-worm eggs – tiny balls of electric green strands in jelly, linked by stalks to the rocks. I discover a rusting ship part, perhaps from the boiler of the *Bellavista*.

Usually we see seaweed at low tide on the shore and jellyfish washed up dead, but under water they come alive. Going a little deeper, I'm surrounded by seaweed and kelp of vivid greens and browns and reds standing up straight and swaying – it's like I'm in a lush forest.

I am exploring a very strange environment, like being in space. It reminds me of the thrill I got the first time I went to a dark nightclub under the railway arches in the city, seeing ornate Goths and pierced metallers; the thrill that I could be among these exotic and tattooed creatures, that it was so easy to walk into a world I'd only ever seen in films and music videos. Under water, I feel like I've gone through the looking glass.

I put my head above the surface and my stomach lurches when I realise I've drifted. It is hard to tell time, distance and direction in the water. I don't know how long I've been in. Due to the refraction of light in water, objects appear larger and closer. Sound travels faster. This distortion interferes with co-ordination. I try to pick up a shell and find my hand clumsily swishing through water.

It doesn't take long for this world to become my new reality. The swaying seaweed is reflected on the underside of the water's surface, which has formed my new sky. It's a grey, overcast day and when I pop my mask up above, I immediately want to get back under water – it's brighter and bigger there. When I do stand up, I feel invincible in the wetsuit, able to walk through nettle patches and wade across lochs. Back home, I peel it off like a selkie's skin.

Anne keeps posting pictures: urchins and father-lashers and lumpsuckers and seven-armed starfish. She hopes to see an octopus or even make Orkney's first record in more than 150 years of a seahorse. She often snorkels in Scapa Flow and says that sometimes she is surrounded by so many swimming and seabed creatures that it feels like being in a fishbowl. I want to learn and see more. The sea has more depth than land and even a small surface area reveals many layers; the possibilities of entering it make Orkney seem many times bigger. 'In Orkney, our forests are under water,' my Polar Bear friend Sam tells me.

There are about a million marine species, with hundreds of thousands still undiscovered. If a rare bird is spotted in Orkney, many people will rush to see it but there is so much still unknown about sea life. Government policy on marine protection zones is still being formulated with more discoveries made all the time.

A recent survey found a puzzling 'faceless, brainless fish-like creature' in waters off the East Mainland.

Papay fisherman Douglas goes out most days, year-round, on his boat *Dawn Harvest*, setting and retrieving creels laid on the seabed around the island to catch lobsters and crabs, which he sells to the shellfish factory in Westray. There used to be three creel boats working around Papay, and before that most crofters would have had a small boat they used to catch fish for their own table and to bolster their meagre incomes.

Out on his boat, Douglas has seen not only minke and right whales and orca, but also sunfish – gigantic, circular fish, like a tractor wheel, with a dorsal fin that pokes above the water. He tells me about fishermen in Westray pulling up a tropical turtle that had become tangled in fishing lines. He tells me about gannets flying, trailing plastic necklaces – they had dived straight through the holes in drink-can packaging. He once pulled up a guillemot that had dived into a creel sitting on the seabed 30 fathoms (55 metres) deep.

Anne has never seen an octopus but Douglas confirms they are in Orkney's waters. Octopus enter the creels while hunting and inject the crabs with poison that pulverises their flesh within the shells. The octopus are clever enough to eat the crab, getting to Douglas's catch before him, leaving him just the shells, then exit the creel and escape.

* * *

Back in the summer, I went searching for bats in one of Orkney's only woods, using a special detector that converts their echo-location into noise audible by humans. There are more dimensions than I thought: frequencies we can't usually hear, habitats we can't normally breathe in. It is thrilling to enter them, just for a short time.

I read about how we might have more than five senses, like the heat sensors in our skin that can tell if something is warm without actually touching it, or how we are able to know if we are upside down.

When I came to Papay, I was attracted to the idea that, by living and walking within its coast, I could become familiar with the whole island and know all of its residents. Small islands are easier to comprehend than cities and I thought I could be able to understand it all. However, I find out about the 'coastline paradox', which explains how it is impossible accurately to measure the length of a coastline. The smaller the scale used to measure, the longer it becomes: a coastline is fractal, breaking into ever smaller inlets and cracks and promontories and bumps, from hundreds of miles to millimetres. This accounts for the vastly different estimates for the length of coastline in Orkney and how, the longer I am on Papay, the more there is to discover. I am thrilled and daunted.

People with longer sober times in AA say that the good things about their new lives are things they didn't imagine, things they couldn't explain to a newcomer. They say that what you think you wanted is likely not, in fact, to be what you want.

I never saw myself as, and resist becoming, the wholesome

'outdoors' type. But the things I experience keep dragging me in. There are moments that thrill and glow: the few seconds a silver male hen harrier flies beside my car one afternoon; the porpoise surfacing around our small boat; the wonderful sight of a herd of cattle let out on grass after a winter indoors, skipping and jumping, tails straight up to the sky with joy.

I am free-falling but grabbing these things as I plunge. Maybe this is what happens. I've given up drugs, don't believe in God and love has gone wrong, so now I find my happiness and flight in the world around me.

Snorkelling is a completely new experience. I enter a new ecosystem, stimulating my thoughts and senses, shaking myself out of sad routine. I feel elated and refreshed afterwards, wanting to tell others of the strange seldom-seen world lying so close to our everyday lives, the secrets under piers and at the edge of car parks.

I've not gone mad. Dad doesn't take any medication to control his manic depression and has not been seriously ill for years. He has found a way to deal with it himself, to recognise the triggers, to know the shifts and the lie of the ocean bed.

Since I got sober, I sometimes find myself surprised and made joyful by normal life. It can feel like a hallucination, this stunning reality. Face down in shallow water, coated in neoprene and breathing through a tube, I feel as if I've opened a door that has always been in my house but I had never noticed. Life can be bigger and richer than I knew.

27

STRANDINGS

IN 1952 THERE WERE WINDS in Orkney so strong they blew away hen houses, killing 70,000 chickens and effectively ending the islands' poultry industry. An account of the storm said 'tethered cows had been flying in the air like kites'.

At primary school, on the windiest days, the smallest children are not allowed outside at playtimes. In the big winds of early December last year, half of one of Dad's cattle-feeders – a six-foot-diameter steel ring – was found five fields away, having crossed fences and dykes. The old chest freezer I liked to shelter behind blew across the field and almost hit the caravan, and the shopping-trolley shelters at Tesco in Kirkwall bent and buckled.

Orkney has a fairly temperate climate, with warmer temperatures than other places on a similar latitude, thanks to the Gulf Stream, but the wind is our most defining weather characteristic, and its relentlessness is often the thing newcomers find hardest to deal with. Farmers battle against the wind, often losing. Dad planted a field of new grass but early gales ripped it out.

The wind, as well as the salty air, is the main reason there are few trees in Orkney and none on the farm. People don't bother with flimsy bird-feeders or greenhouses that would be gone in the first gale, and umbrellas are rare. This year, the Papay Christmas tree is sunk in concrete: the last few blew over.

Because I grew up in it, I like the wind: it makes me excited, as it does the calves in the field, frisky in blustery weather. It gives me energy, like a fire. I remember power cuts, lights and TV flickering, torches and candles, school closed. In an easterly gale on Papay, waves and spume come over the top of Fowl Craig. I go for a short walk and return ears aching, mania whipped. A small burn is being blown backwards, water rising in a vapour catching the light. The weather-vane on my house has given up and is simply spinning.

The original Beaufort scale didn't give wind speed in miles per hour but, rather, in terms of its effects on sailing ships, from 'just sufficient to give steerage' to 'that which no canvas sails could withstand'. This winter I am having adventures in the Beaufort scale, in the gusts and squalls of the North Isles. On Papay and the Outrun, we are fully exposed to the Atlantic and closest to the passage of areas of low pressure. Here, wind is not just the movement of air caused by changes in pressure in the atmosphere, but a way of life.

There are easterly gales forecast tonight, rising to storm force. I look at the weather-monitoring websites – the Met Office and

Dave Wheeler – and am thrilled by the steeply climbing wind-speed graphs and the area of red coming towards Orkney. The ferry from Kirkwall to Papay is cancelled but the afternoon plane still comes. I watch it land, approaching into the wind, wobbling slightly.

From inside by the fire, I feel the air pressure drop and hear the wind rise. It is suddenly howling and whistling around Rose Cottage in different tones, like an orchestra tuning up. I go outside for thirty seconds to retrieve the bird-feeder and return with my face salty from sea spray.

Orkney folk will usually only go as far as saying it's 'a bit blowy', but tonight everyone on the internet admits that it's 'blowin' a whoolie'. Tonight Orcadians are battening down their hen houses, predicting that wheelie bins and trampolines will be flying in the town. I speak to Dad, who's in the caravan at the farm – he's staying there tonight 'in case the roof starts to come off'.

At five o'clock, the height of the storm, the window of the caravan blew in. A whirlwind was created inside, lifting the farm paperwork. Objects that had been with Dad since we lived in the farmhouse – pictures and furniture – shook and fell. There was a storm inside his house. Dad opened the door to relieve the pressure and managed to drag a sheet of plywood to cover the window, a temporary solution.

Two mornings later, after the storm has subsided, there is fear mixed with intrigue on Papay. What has it done? I'm still here but my crate of driftwood outside the house has shifted. I retrieve the lid of my compost bin from a field over the road.

I walk the east coast of the island to see if anything good has been washed up. The combination of east winds and high tides was unusual. The variables of wind, pressure, the state of the tide, currents and rainfall had combined to cause much damage on the shore.

Some sand dunes had been breached, with waves blowing onto the front road. The water has now subsided but rocks, seaweed and other debris are strewn over the track. At North Wick, there are huge piles of seaweed where two days ago there were none. What was a gentle slope from the dunes down onto the beach is now a tall step. Tonnes of sand have been moved and rocks exposed.

Over on North Ronaldsay, more than 2,000 metres of the famous dyke for keeping the native sheep on the shore to graze seaweed were washed away, causing the worst damage in seventy-five years. On Shapinsay, an amazing array of fish – tadpole fish, ling, young cod, saithe, cuckoo wrasse and ballan wrasse – were washed up on a boaty noust, stranded when the tide surged.

Continuing on my walk, at the old kelp store, nestled by the door beside a concrete block, is a seal pup. I stop and we stare at each other for a few moments before it snarls. A couple of adult seals are in the sea nearby and I want them to call to the youngster.

I ring island wildlife expert Tim for advice. It is likely that the pup was washed over here from the nearby uninhabited island of Faray, where grey seals breed, and has been separated from its mother. This may have been its first attempt at swimming. It still has its white baby fur but some sharp teeth too, meaning it might be able to fend for itself in the sea.

The pup is still there the next morning but Tim manages to drag it back into the sea on a sack. It swims off strongly to take its chances in the wild.

A few years ago, I drunkenly got into an argument with someone I shouldn't have. She retorted by calling me 'washed-up'. It stung because at that point it was fairly true. I was out of work, living in a tiny room in east London, not getting invited out, heart-broken and drinking alone. My once promising future, for which I'd moved to London, was turning into bitterness and frustration. My options were ever-decreasing and I didn't know where to turn, desperately seeking comfort in sexual encounters and obses-sive memories. My life had become unmanageable.

When I first came back to Orkney I felt like the strandings of jellyfish, laid out on the rocks for all to see. I was washed-up: no longer buoyant, battered and storm-tossed.

I think of the things I have lost: my compass, stolen laptop, two shoes – one in the canal, one out of the door of a moving car – my boyfriend. But I also think of the things I have found from the sea: the fishing boat, the seal, the 'ambergris'. These things were worn out and washed-up but they were not always useless. They had tales to tell.

One Sunday morning while I am on Papay, a highly unusual animal washes onto the beach on North Ronaldsay: a walrus. These huge sea beasts, north Atlantic walruses, are more usually found in Greenland and north Norway and none had been seen in Orkney since 1986. Every islander goes out to see it, huge, tusked, posing obligingly on the beach, while wildlife enthusiasts and photographers book themselves on the first plane. By nightfall it has dragged itself back into the water and swum north. A few days later the same animal, distinguishable by its markings, is spotted on the Norwegian coastline.

When beachcombing, I get used to noticing and homing in on anything that looks a bit different among the pebbles, caught in a rockpool or buried in the sand. Usually it's a piece of plastic – a drink bottle, one flip-flop, a crisps packet from 1993, bits of fish crate. These fragments of junk are so numerous and non-perishable that they are a serious threat to bird and sea life. But the idea of 'rubbish' is subjective. Anne uses sea-smoothed broken glass for her jewellery; I burn driftwood.

Today something catches my eye in the tangles. I pick up a tiny – it would fit in a matchbox – headless, handless, footless porcelain figurine: a grisly find. I give it a rinse in a rockpool. It is white and naked with a protruding tummy and bottom.

During a gale in 1868 a ship called the *Lessing*, on its way from Bremerhaven in Germany to New York, drove into the rocks at Klavers Geo on Fair Isle. All 465 passengers, emigrants hoping to start a new life in the United States, and crew were brought safely ashore by the islanders but the ship itself was broken up by the sea and its cargo, including china dolls, dispersed. A figurine from the wreck in the Shetland Museum looks tantalisingly similar in style to my find.

I like to think my figurine, now in my pocket with the Westray Wife, came from the wreck. For years it might have been buried in the seabed but a perfect combination of time elapsed, stormy seas, east winds and high tides brought it for me to find on this spot on Papay this winter.

There is a cycle. The things we put into the sea come back to us – parts of the crushed car will be washed up again – but because the ocean is downhill from everywhere, they will go back there eventually. I wonder if I might find the shoe I lost in the London canal on an Orkney shore. As my time on Papay comes to an end, I am untethered and free-floating, like the jellyfish. I am wondering what's next, standing back and allowing the unexpected to wash up at my feet.

I've been holding my breath. I've been clenching my teeth. I've been searching the seashore, each day, just looking for a moment when I can feel at ease. I run my tongue over the tooth that's chipped from opening beer bottles. Although it's smoother now, the chip will always be there. I rub the scar on the back of my head. Deep in the night, I still think of my ex-boyfriend and how I didn't change in time to save our relationship. He lives in America now, with his girlfriend, and I heard they have a baby.

People like to tell me I'm looking 'well' but there are late hours alone when my heart is an open wound and I wonder if the pain will ever stop brimming fresh. I cannot smooth out the fault line. At these times, drink suggests itself as a solution. 'Getting sober' is not a moment after which everything gets better but an ongoing and slow process of rebuilding with regular setbacks, wobbles and temptations.

One morning after a bad night, walking on the east side of Papay, I see a plastic bottle among the rocks. I pick it up: a Finnish vodka bottle carried from Scandinavia with about a shot's worth left inside. I open it and take a deep smell. The hollow tang of teenage parties, plastic cups in dark discos and finishing the bottle down an alleyway. An impulse pulling at something deep within me, something strong, tells me to swig it down, all mixed with seawater and sailor spit. Sometimes I think it would just be *funny* to say, 'Fuck it, fuck all of this.' A part of me, when I hear that someone has 'drunk themselves to death', finds the idea attractive: they did it to themselves, they were free. The vodka smell is making me light-headed. It seems so perfect, this mouthful of oblivion sent from the sea.

But everything I've found in the past year is pulling me more strongly: the clear eyes and shooting stars, the fresh mornings when sleep has made me feel better rather than worse. The strength I feel when I end a day without having inebriated myself is true freedom. I screw the cap back on, throw the bottle down and laugh loudly and wildly out into the waves. Is this all you've got, North Sea? I can take it. I can take anything you throw at me.

I stride onwards. The plane passes above and to the passengers I am a lone figure in waterproofs walking the coastline, morning after morning, miles from anywhere, at the north of nowhere. But down here, inside myself, I feel powerful and determined. I am saved from the sea, seeing the beauty in the breakers that almost dragged me under, drinking the cold air with gratitude.

28

RENEWABLES

T HE OUTRUN IS A BIT tucked away, lying on the coast over a low hill, not seen from many houses or the road. It is partly for this reason that it has been chosen as the 'preferred site' to build a huge substation to serve the tidal- and wave-energy devices proposed to be tethered to the seabed at sites off the West Mainland.

The strong winds, big waves and powerful tides of the islands are a natural resource. Our location between the Atlantic and the North Sea, and the way water moves between islands, means there are strong and fast-flowing currents around Orkney: our waters are potentially energy rich.

There is a history on the islands of harnessing these natural forces for power. Watermills were used for grinding grain in the nineteenth century and before. On Papay, until about 1930, the threshing of grain was done by a 'windy gear' when a sail drove the mill. Islanders have made their living from the sea in different ways over the centuries: fishing and whaling, transport and leisure, the offshore oil industry. This new industry of 'renewable power' is another way of using local resources, skills, knowledge and equipment.

The Scottish government has an ambitious target to have renewable sources generating 100 per cent of Scotland's gross annual electricity consumption by 2020. In a world running out of fossil fuels and trying to emit less carbon dioxide into the atmosphere, Orkney, hailed as a 'global centre' for these technologies, provides hope.

Over the last decade, local councillors, business people and visiting politicians have talked of the economic benefits of renewable energy for Orkney, like those the oil industry and Flotta have provided for the last forty years. The developments will require huge infrastructure changes, and new piers are being built to support the burgeoning industry, allowing large service vessels to come ashore.

Orkney is home to the European Marine Energy Centre (EMEC), where researchers develop new technologies. Out at sea, off the West Mainland, devices are being tested to harness tidal and wave power. The Pelamis 'sea snake' contains oil-filled pumps that convert the motion of waves to create electricity and the Oyster devices use pressurised water to drive generators.

On land, one of the biggest changes I noticed when I returned to Orkney from London was the wind turbines now dotted across the islands. Orkney now has 25 per cent of the UK's small wind turbines and most farms have one. The structures are our modern-day standing stones, cutting vertically across Orkney's horizontal landscape, painted a specific shade of grey developed to be most unobtrusive in bleak Scottish skies.

Scores of representatives from energy companies have visited Dad in his caravan and walked up to the Outrun, carrying out geological, environmental and engineering surveys. They show Dad maps and, with the suggestion of large sums of money floating in the air, explain their plans.

The seabed around Orkney belongs to the Crown Estate and, after a tender process, areas have been leased to different energy companies. The Crown Estate has set developers the target of generating 1.2 gigawatts of electricity by 2020 – sufficient for around 750,000 homes. In thirteen seabed sites off the West Mainland, scores of wave-top power devices are proposed to be tethered.

Huge cables will, they suggest, be drilled through the cliff, coming out just below sea level, joining the substation to the devices. The substation will gather the energy before passing it on to the National Grid, as well as providing access to construct, install and service the machines.

In mid-January, on the shore just beyond the farm, by the rock-pools where we swim, an enormous metal octagon weighing several tonnes was found by a neighbour, wedged in some rocks.

It is one of the 'doughnuts' made and installed by a renewable-energy company, designed to float on top of the water, tethered to a foundation on the seabed. The floats move up and down, converting wave motion into pressurised water, which is pumped ashore to drive hydroelectric turbines to produce electricity.

The tethers were designed to withstand great force but something was rubbing up against them, causing them to snap – and the doughnuts were carried away by the sea.

The big problem is that the developers still haven't made test devices that work over a sustained period. These multi-million-pound contraptions keep breaking up, smashed and twisted by the ocean. Orcadians are unsurprised. I have seen that the sea has enough power to throw a seal over a fence and to change the appearance of a mile-long beach over a weekend's storm.

Onshore, the concern is that the parts of wind turbines will rust and break, not withstand the power of the wind and corrosion that have always plagued these islands, and have to be replaced before they have earned their projected profits or even before they've paid for their own construction. On Papay the community-owned wind turbine was, ironically, blown down.

These huge experimental feats of engineering, worked on by the top minds in science, were overcome by the very tugs and flows of the waves, currents and winds they were meant to harness. Tonnes of sea junk were washed back onto the land they came from, bashed up and sorry-looking.

The same strong seas that are proclaimed as the reason why Orkney is a good location for wave and tidal energy are also the forces that make it difficult. The date for improving the cable links to take power to the National Grid keeps being pushed back, and the future of marine energy in Orkney for anything but testing is uncertain.

I grew up in some extremes and later sought them for myself, unconsciously emulating unremembered experiences. Now, I still pursue heightened states but do so with greater self-knowledge. I want to have a story but I have to do it sober. I am choosing strength and beauty and creation. Like the electricity devices, I'm trying to find the right way to harness the powers and to achieve my aims without being destroyed by the very energy I desire.

One reason alcohol is addictive is that it doesn't quite work. It's difficult to get enough of something that almost works. It temporarily gave some relief so I chased it, again and again, my Fata Morgana, and it made me feel worse. For me, alcohol had become a mirage. It wasn't a solution but I hoped it was going to be and kept returning to it, desperately.

When I am experiencing the impulse to drink, I try to examine it further, that false promise. I am experiencing discomfort and want something to provide flow and easiness. I want something to take the edge off. But I'm realising that times of anxiety are necessary and unavoidable and, in any case, I like the edge: it's where I get my best ideas. The edge is where I'm from. It's my home.

Drinking solves nothing. Afterwards, the problems are still

there. In London, I was hiding from my life and family in Orkney, breaking up, and trying to escape. By coming back I faced it and now Orkney is trying to keep me. People are kind and offer opportunities. There are geos and headlands and islands I haven't visited yet. The music and voices of the isles simultaneously make my heart swell and make me want to take the next ferry out.

I'm not sure what's next. Maybe after this winter on Papay, picnicking behind dykes, I'll return to London for a while, dining on the fortieth floor of a City skyscraper. I've swung from active alcoholism to strict sobriety, from inner city to outer isle. I seek pure sensation, just as an octopus can taste with all of its skin. I feel good alone and going somewhere.

The developers are interested in buying a hundred acres of land – sixty-two from Dad, including most of the Outrun, and the rest from neighbouring farms. Two huge buildings are planned, each with a footprint of ten acres. Even if the farmers don't want to sell, the development is important enough potentially to force a compulsory purchase order.

I've returned to the islands at exciting times. I am generally in favour of renewable energy. This is a new way of using the land and our natural resources, providing income for the islands into the twenty-first century and reducing our use of fossil fuels, as well as giving a one-off cash boost to ageing farmers. But the idea that this beautiful, barely touched stretch of land where I grew up, where I chased lambs, watched birds and hid with my brother, should become an industrial zone is dizzying. Computer-modelled plans pull at my memories and emotions. Dad and neighbouring farmers are in limbo.

Things change and move on. For me, the way the farm was when I was a child was lost when Mum left and the house was sold. The Outrun could be sold for the substation but the waves will still crash indifferently up against its cliffs. The engineers laying the cables will feel the tremors. The same wind that whistles through the windows of my peedie pink house will turn the blade of turbines, cutting the air in an endless pattern.

Spring is coming, guillemots are returning to the cliffs at Fowl Craig and the RSPB warden will soon be back, so it is time for me to leave Papay. I choose to leave not by plane but more slowly, on the steamer.

The spring equinox is soon: I will be two years' sober. Although I mainly rely on my own forms of therapy – walking, swimming – I have started going through the rest of the 12 Steps, designed to be a programme for sustainable living. Step Nine is to make 'amends' with those people we have harmed. I write my ex-boyfriend a letter that I will not send but keep in my bag in case I meet him again. I get a text from the girl, my peer, who was in the psychiatric ward telling me she's got to ninety days' sober – a significant milestone in AA – for the first time and has been accepted to become a student nurse.

The forces that I grew up with are being utilised in unexpected ways. Recovery is making use of something once thought worthless. I might have been washed-up but I can be renewed. In these two years I have put my energy into searching for elusive corncrakes, Merry Dancers and rare cloud; into swimming in cold seas, running naked around stone circles, sailing to abandoned islands, flying on tiny planes, coming back home.

I'm on my way to see my toddler nephew Joe, who was born shortly after I got sober. He will never see me drunk. I feel powerful. I expect more from myself than I would wish on others. At night I have visions, perfectly conjured spaces and memories: every window I've ever smoked out of and all my favourite songs; all the parties I've been to and forgotten; a stone X I saw from the plane, built so that sheep can shelter from wind blowing from all directions. I wake in the night and experience an instant of raised consciousness, a new state that is to 'awake' what awake is to sleep.

Rain on me. Strike me with fire. I feel like lightning in slow motion. I am one fathom deep and contain the unknown. I am vibrating at a frequency invisible to man and I'm ready to be brave. From the upper saloon of the MV *Thorfinn*, I watch Papay disappear over the horizon. The last two years stretch and glitter behind me like the wake of the ferry. The powers are churning inside me.

ACKNOWLEDGEMENTS

M Y THANKS, FOR SUPPORT AND inspiration in many ways, go to Jeremy Allen, Fong Chau, Cate Finlayson, Amelia Green, Jenni Fagan, Henrik Hedinge, Katharine Hibbert, Karen Hinckley, Mira Manga, Sarah Perry, John Rogers, Dee Quintas, Dave Wheeler, Sam and all the staff and peers of the Island Day Programme, everyone at RSPB Orkney, Orkney Polar Bear Club, my Twitter and Facebook friends, and the people of Papay.

I was lucky to have readers who helped with the manuscript at various stages. Thank you, Tristan Burke, Mathew Clayton, Patrick Hussey, Karen Hinckley, John McGill and Malachy Tallack. I'm also grateful for the care and enthusiasm of my agent, James MacDonald Lockhart of Antony Harwood Ltd, and my editor at Canongate, Jenny Lord.

My special thanks go to Robin Turner, Jeff Barrett and Andrew Walsh, who published some early parts of this material on the wonderful Caught by the River website and encouraged me to develop it.

During my time on Papay I was supported by, and am highly grateful for, an artist's bursary from Creative Scotland.

With love to my family, this book is for you: Jane, John, Dorothy, Tom, Peggy, Joseph and Stella.

A NOTE ON THE TYPE

THIS BOOK IS SET IN Bembo, a humanist serif typeface commissioned by Aldus Manutius and cut by Francesco Griffo, a Venetian goldsmith, in the late fifteenth century.

This harmonious typeface has gone on to inspire generations of type founders, from Claude Garamond in the sixteenth century to Stanley Morison at the Monotype Corporation in the early twentieth century.